Old Father William's
Well-Ordered
Universe

Bert - happy B.D. 2009
This is the kind of
book Monsignor
McCabe would write -
enjoy - the Pawleys

Old Father William's Well-Ordered Universe

A Generally Reliable Compendium of
Facts, Figures, and Formulae, Specifically Intended for the
Bathroom Bound (and Those Who Love Them)

Bill Richardson

Collins

Old Father William's Well-Ordered Universe
© 2008 by Bill Richardson. All rights reserved.

Hand-drawn illustrations © 2008 by Charles Checketts. All rights reserved.

Published by Collins, an imprint of HarperCollins Publishers Ltd.

First edition

Excerpt on page 159 from *Bear Attacks: Their Causes and Avoidance,* New Revised Edition
by Stephen Herrero © 1985, 2003. Published by McClelland & Stewart Ltd.
Used with permission of the publisher.

Excerpts on pages xiii, 57, 113, and 227 are from *Alice's Adventures in Wonderland*
by Lewis Carroll, accompanied by illustrations by Sir John Tenniel.

HarperCollins books may be purchased for educational, business,
or sales promotional use through our Special Markets Department.

HarperCollins Publishers Ltd
2 Bloor Street East, 20th Floor
Toronto, Ontario, Canada
M4W 1A8

www.harpercollins.ca

Library and Archives Canada Cataloguing in Publication

Richardson, Bill, 1955–
Old Father William's well-ordered universe : a generally reliable
compendium of facts, figures, and formulae, specifically intended for
the bathroom bound (and those who love them) / Bill Richardson.

ISBN 978-1-55468-024-5

1. Curiosities and wonders. 2. Canadian wit and humor (English). I. Title.

AG106.R43 2008   031.02   C2008-901906-7

WEB 9 8 7 6 5 4 3 2 1

Printed and bound in Canada

To Billy

Contents

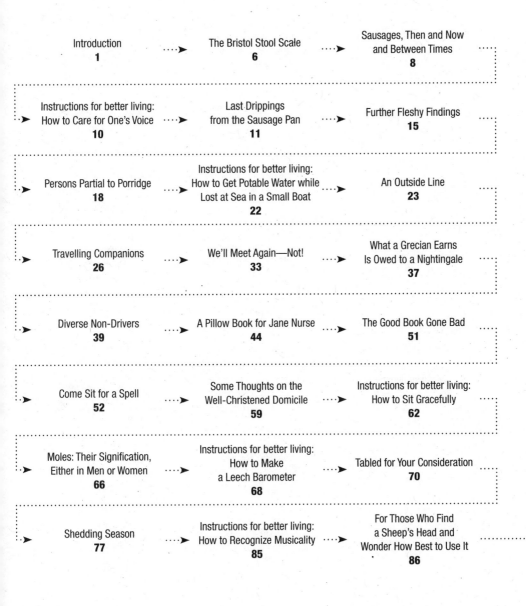

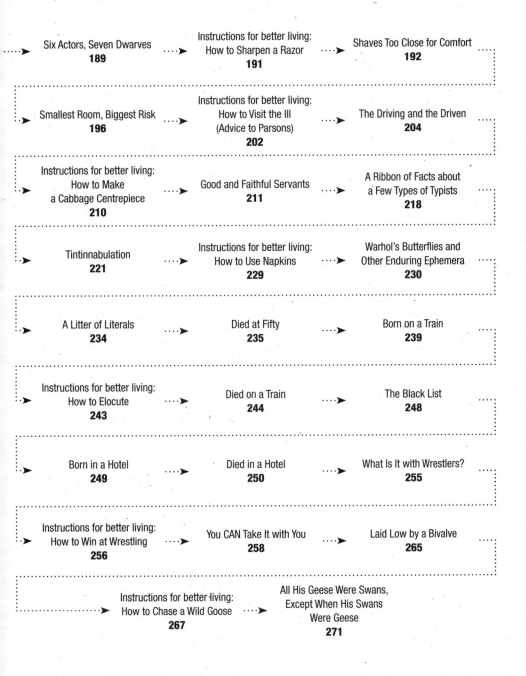

"You are old, Father William," the young man said,
"And your hair has become very white,
And yet you incessantly stand on your head—
Do you think, at your age, it is right?"

"In my youth," Father William replied to his son,
"I feared it might injure the brain;
But now that I'm perfectly sure I have none,
Why, I do it again and again."

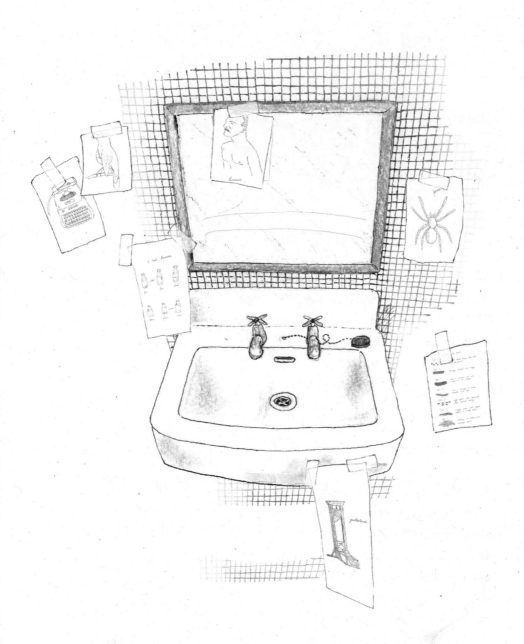

Old Father William's Natural Habitat

Introduction

Old Father William, what a silly man,
All day, all night, never leaves the can.
Old Father William, what a tiny tomb,
All day, all night, in the smallest room.
Old Father William, living all alone,
All day, all night, perched upon the throne.

History of necessity repeats itself. The number of anecdotes in its reper-
toire is vast, but not bottomless. Hence it happens, sometimes, while
considering the historical record, that you'll discover an aspect of the
past so much in sync with your own circumstances that you'll wonder if the
script of your life, which you'd thought was original, is just some fusty old scenario, recycled from a melodrama of yore. I myself am channelling, seemingly,
the spirit of a minor character from the past's rich and redundant pageant.
When I study the facts of the case of one Henry Welby, I can only conclude that
he and Old Father William are as one. *Henri Welby, c'est moi.*

Welby's life and work were described in a pamphlet published in 1637 under
the anything-but-brisk title *The Phoenix of these late Times; or the Life of Henry
Welby, Esq., who lived at his House, in Grub Street, Forty four years, and in that
Space was never seen by any: And there died, Oct. 29, 1636, aged Eighty four.
Shewing the first Occasion and Reason thereof. With Epitaphs and Elegies on the
late Deceased Gentleman; who lyeth buried in St. Giles' Church, near Cripplegate,
London.* This tract discloses how Henry—"the hermit of Grub Street" as he is
better known—retired from the world after a violent quarrel with his brother.
Driven over the edge by family treachery—and with no reality television as a

reference point and no group therapy into which he could channel his angst—he opted for hermithood. He sold off his estate, which was large, moved to the city, and took a modest house in the Cripplegate neighbourhood of London. There he spent the next forty-four years, seeing no one save his faithful old servant, Elizabeth. She died—worn out, one imagines, from tending to the anchorite's needs—and Henry followed along a few days later. Then, as now, good help must have been hard to find.

I consider his peculiar tale and feel the creepy wash of déjà vu; for between the Venn diagrams of our lives, Henry's and mine, there are significant points of coincidence. Mind you, he has better third-party documentation than I will ever be accorded. I am remembered only in the skipping rhymes that sometimes filter through my shuttered windows from the street outside:

Old Father William, dusk turns into dawn,
All day, all night, hiding in the john.
Old Father William, must be getting stiff,
All day, all night, cramped up in the biff.
Old Father William, oh for goodness' sake,
Come out, come out, come out of the jakes.

I can't recall exactly when or why I made my own Welbyesque retreat and became the object of such crude, if accurate, fun. There was no specific trigger, such as the one that fired Henry into distraction's bull's eye. It didn't happen all at once, that much is sure. It was a gradual shrinking, such as the better garments enjoy. Slowly, slowly, without even noticing that it was underway, I commenced my withdrawal from society. I would look up from my reading and realize that a day or two had gone by and I hadn't left the house. Then a week, a fortnight, a month would pass and I wouldn't stir, save for when the cat food ran low, a letter needed posting, or a creditor howled loudly enough to warrant appeasing. There was nothing desperate about this, nothing determined or deliberate. It simply became my way. Over time, it dawned that I needed less and less of all the many things I had once seen as necessary. Money. Company. Food. Space. What did I want all these rooms for? What did I want that bed for,

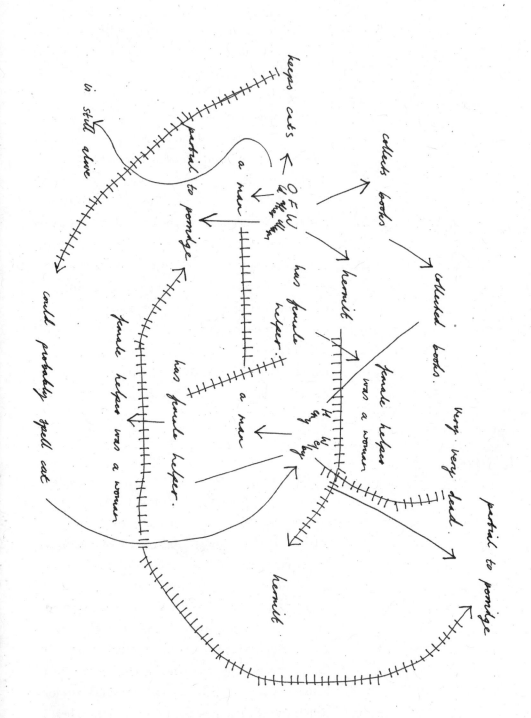

Traffic Pattern at the Intersection of Welby and William

when I could stretch out quite nicely in the tub? What need had I of all those chairs when I had a perfectly commodious commode with a porcelain tank that is entirely adequate as a desk?

I placed a call to Meals on Wheels and was put in touch with a kindly volunteer named Jane Nurse. I arranged with her for a now-and-again delivery of kibble and litter and my own rudimentary comestibles. Like any good recluse, I'm mostly partial to pulses and simples and weak broths and suchlike fare: the nutritive equivalent of the hair shirt. I explained to my seven pussies where they could find me, if necessary. Then I picked up my hot plate, an all-purpose cauldron, and a good supply of reading material, and—like one of those prehistoric Scandinavian hunters whose remains occasionally surface from a drying marsh—I installed myself in the bog. I've been there ever since. I am there now.

•

"When found, make a note of," says Captain Cuttle in Dickens's *Dombey and Son*. This excellent advice has become my call to arms. And while Captain Cuttle is a model for me, so too are Jack Kerouac and the Marquis de Sade. Kerouac, you'll recall, wrote *On the Road* on a single 120-foot roll of paper, and the jolly old Marquis used a similar method to write the *120 Days of Sodom,* a twelve-metre scroll that could be rolled up and hidden from his jailers in the Bastille. I, Old Father William, keep my records on the rolls available to me. Single-ply is fine, and ballpoint works best. I read, I make a note of, I rip, I post, and I look for patterns to emerge. Why am I thus engaged? For no good reason, save that one must do what one can with what one has to make some sense of the world. Old Father William says that retreat from society doesn't absolve one of one's responsibilities as a citizen. This is just my little way of contributing. And now and again, I write a letter or two and launch my found pebbles into the big pond of the beyond. If you hear from here the sound of *plop, plop, plop,* that is all it is. If some of these ripples reach your particular shore, it won't have been in vain. Your faithful, if somewhat peculiar servant, I remain,

Old Father William, scribbling in the loo,
Take this, read this, it is meant for you.

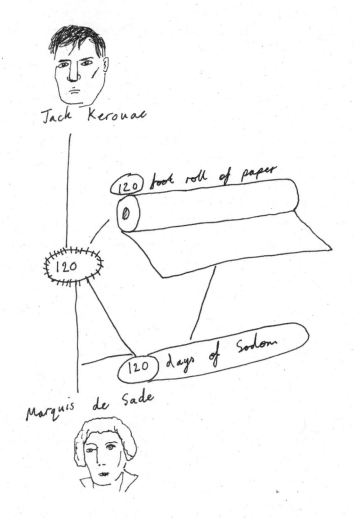

The Bristol Stool Scale

Were I in a situation where I could be more Nobel than noble, the first recipients of the Old Father William Prize would surely be K.W. Heaton and S.J. Lewis. It was their research into "intestinal transit time" (see the *Scandinavian Journal of Gastroenterology,* volume 32, issue 9, 1997) that made possible the Bristol Stool Scale. Humanity advances only when someone, somewhere, understands that a gap needs filling, a hole requires plugging. It was the particular genius of Heaton and Lewis to intuit that all the world was waiting, not just for the sunrise but also for a seven-part parsing of fecal output.

Here at Dude Cottage, we refer to this chart constantly. Should future scholars, when studying the Old Father William diaries, be perplexed by the inclusion of such annotations as "a perfect 3" or "verging on 4, very comfy" or "a rare 2.5 episode today," they need look no further than the Bristol Stool Scale for elucidation. The illustrations are, as is evident, very telling, but the tender descriptions also clutch at the heart. "Soft blobs with clear-cut edges." "Fluffy pieces with ragged edges, a mushy stool." Excellent writing! And such clever use of the sausage as metaphor, too; so much more savoury, I think, than "like a cigar." My own life's work can be described in sausagey terms. What do I do, after all, but gather and stuff and make link after link after link? Linkage is Old Father William's raison d'être.

The Bristol Stool Scale

Type 1

Separate hard lumps, like nuts
(hard to pass)

Type 2

Sausage-shaped but lumpy

Type 3

Like a sausage but with
cracks on its surface.

Type 4

Like a sausage or snake
smooth and soft

Type 5

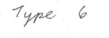

Soft blobs with clear-cut
edges (passed easily)

Type 6

Fluffy pieces with ragged
edges, a mushy stool.

Type 7

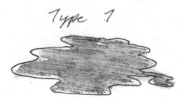

Watery, no solid pieces.
Entirely liquid

Sausages,
Then and Now and Between Times

Constantine the Great banned sausages, in the very early years of the Christian era, on the assumption that the eating of them led to immorality. He may have had a point. Consider how, on July 9, 2003, Miss Mandy Block was assaulted by Pittsburgh Pirates first baseman Randall Simon while she was dressed as an Italian sausage and taking part in a mascot race against a hot dog, a bratwurst, and a Polish sausage. Mr. Simon whacked her as she raced past the dugout. He was cuffed, fined, and suspended for three games.

•

In Manchester, on August 11, 2007, a twelve-year-old boy was taken into police custody for throwing what was believed to be a stone at Michael Deegan, a seventy-four-year-old pensioner. The missile, which struck Mr. Deegan in the shoulder, proved to be a cocktail sausage.

•

The cocktail sausage arrest in Manchester led to much editorializing about police excesses. But where was that boy in April 2005, when a driver, moving at speed along an English motorway, was struck in the face by an object that entered the window of his car and broke his nose? The object was a frozen sausage. Old Father William senses a pattern emerging.

•

In 2006, police in Zwickau, Germany, arrested a man on the suspicion that he was somehow behind the demise of a sixty-five-year-old woman who had choked to death on a large piece of bockwurst. Quite how the accused might have involved himself in this asphyxiation was not made specific. A dare, foolishly taken? Amateur hypnosis gone badly wrong? Old Father William would love to know.

•

Death by sausage sounds like a plot point from an Agatha Christie novel. Christie said of her productivity, "I am like a sausage machine. As soon as [I finish a novel] and cut off the string, I have to think of the next one."

•

The Sausage Tree, which grows in Africa, is so called because its fruit resembles a you-know-what. It can be three feet long and weigh as much as twenty pounds—the fruit, that is—and presumably, one wouldn't want to be reading one's Kipling under such a tree when the fruit chose to detach itself from the branch and prove Newton's point, yet again.

•

Speaking of Kipling, we find in his story "Reingelder and the German Flag" the sausage metaphor used in a charmingly vernacular way: "Dere is one snake howefer dot we who gollect know ash der Sherman Flag, pecause id is red und plack und white, joost like a sausage mit druffles."

Joost like a sausage mit druffles: a phrase that would not be out of place on the Bristol Stool Scale.

•

Once, during a performance of *La Bohème,* Enrico Caruso, in a prank-playing mood, pressed a hot sausage into the palm of Dame Nellie Melba during the famous "Che Gelida Manina" aria, in which Rodolfo sings to Mimi about her cold little hands. History has not deigned to record how the Australian diva responded. If she knew the Italian for "**bastard**," however, we can pretty much guess.

Bastard, 10 ways

Croatian	kopile
Dutch	bastaard
Farsi	harazadeh
French	salaud
German	Hurensohn
Hungarian	fattyú
Icelandic	óskilgetið barn
Italian	bastardo
Spanish	cabrón
Welsh	blentyn gordderch

9

Instructions for better living

HOW TO CARE FOR ONE'S VOICE

Let me give you one of my greatest secrets. Like all secrets, it is perfectly simple and rational. Never give to the public all you have. That is, the singer owes it to herself never to go to the boundaries of her vocal possibilities. The singer who sings to the utmost every time would be like the athlete who exhausted himself to the state of collapse. This is the only way in which I can account for what the critics term 'the remarkable preservation' of my own voice. I have been singing for years in all parts of the world, growing richer in musical experience, and yet my voice to-day feels as fresh and clear as when I was in my teens.

—Dame Nellie Melba, "A Talk with the Girl Who Would Be a Prima Donna"
(*Etude* magazine, January 1914)

Last Drippings
from the Sausage Pan

Dr. J.W.L. Thudicum (see *Namesake Specula*) in his unjustly forgotten book *Cookery: Its Art and Practice* (1895) begins Chapter 60, "Preparations of Pork, the Flesh of the Encyclopaedic Animal," with this truism: "It has been truly said that without pork there would be no bacon, and without bacon no accomplished cookery." And in their book *Perfumes: The Guide* (2008), Luca Turin and Tania Sanchez note, "The question that women casually shopping for perfume ask more than any other is, 'What scent drives a man wild?' After years of intensive research, we know the definitive answer. It is bacon."

The Ideal Bacon Sandwich

$$N = C + \{f_b(c_m) \cdot f_b(t_c)\} + f_b(T_s) + f_c \cdot t_a$$

This is the formula devised by a team of British scientists to express the ideal bacon sandwich. Graham Clayton, speaking on behalf of the team that worked for over a thousand hours on the study and tested seven hundred variants, said that Danish bacon was best suited to sandwich use, and explained that the formula uses the following values:

N = breaking strain, in newtons, of cooked bacon
f_b = function of the bacon type
f_c = function of the condiment or filling effect
T_s = serving temperature
t_c = cooking time
t_a = time taken to insert the condiment or filling
c_m = cooking method
C = breaking strain, in newtons, of uncooked bacon

{
What scent drives a man wild?
We know the definitive answer. It is bacon.
}

In that same month, same year, and same country, a collection of oddments long since discarded by the English painter Francis Bacon, but cleverly gathered up and preserved by an electrician with an eye to their future worth, sold at Sotheby's for £965,490. Among the items auctioned was a study for a painting of a painter: Bacon's friend Lucien Freud.

•

On September 12, 1977, in a taxi city-bound from Kennedy Airport, the American poet Robert Lowell died while clutching a portrait by Lucien Freud. The likeness was of a woman to whom both Freud and Lowell had been married, although at different times: the writer and Guinness heiress Caroline Blackwood (see *Died in a Hotel*). Lowell had just returned from Ireland, where he'd travelled to formally end his marriage to Blackwood, his third wife. He and his second wife, the writer Elizabeth Hardwick, intended to reconcile; it was to her house he was being ferried when his heart gave out.

•

Caroline Blackwood and Lucien Freud met at a party where, when Princess Margaret sat down at the piano and began to sing "Let's Do It," she was shouted down by Francis Bacon. It all comes together, friends, if only you wait it out.

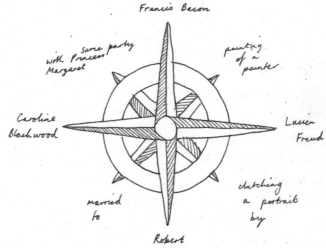

Six Degrees of Francis Bacon

I

Dear Old Father William,

One of your cats—ginger, torn ears—has developed the habit of meeting me when I arrive with my delivery. He sits on the fence and as I approach he turns and presents his butt end to me for inspection. I'm sure it's kindly meant. I found this piece of tissue appended to his posterior orifice. Is it yours, by any chance? It looks to be covered with many notes pertaining to sausages. By the way, did you know that "Sausages in Literature" is a recognized subject heading in the Library of Congress Classification System?

Yours,
Jane Nurse

Dear Jane Nurse,

Thank you for retrieving these notes. They are important to me. And may I express thanks on behalf of the cats, too. I wish I could tell you they would say so themselves, if only they could talk, but that's not the case. Tabby, calico, tortoiseshell, or cream, they're dyed-in-the-wool ingrates. Perhaps you would be interested in the following.

O.F.W.

Further Fleshy Findings

D r. Thudicum, on whose *Cookery: Its Art and Practice* I rely to a remark-able extent—given that the art of cookery is nothing I could be said to practise—also informs us:

> Roast Sucking-Pig was formerly a much more popular dish than it is now; thus, the citizens of London consumed in the year 1725 no less than 52,000 of these animals. It may be stuffed and baked at the baker's, or it may be boned and made into a galantine, with aspic, and served as an entremets. The variations are numerous and very elegant; in many parts of the South sucking-pig is frequently prepared for unexpected guests. The sucking-pig's feet are called petty toes, and worked in a ragout with the pluck and blood of the animal.

•

Meanwhile, Reverend Brewer, LLD, in his typically unimpeachable *Reader's Handbook* of 1911, reminds us that

> James I, returning from a hunting expedition, so much enjoyed his din-ner, consisting of a loin of roast beef, that he laid his sword across it and dubbed it Sir Loin. At Chingford, in Essex, is a place called "Friday Hill House," in one of the rooms of which is an oak table with a brass plate let into it inscribed with the following words: All lovers of roast beef will like to know that on this table a loin was knighted by King James the First on his return from hunting in the Epping Forest. The tradition is that James said, "Bring hither that sur-loin, sirrah, for it is worthy of a more honourable post, being, as I may say, not sur-loin but Sir-loin, the noblest joint of all."

Old Father William has his own recollection of "the noblest joint of all," but it's one of those stories from the sixties that's best left to lie.

•

On October 25, 1809, to celebrate the Jubilee Year of George III, the burghers (not burgers) of the city of Norwich assembled at St. Andrew's Hall for a roast beef dinner. Thomas Preston, in his very odd book *Jubilee Jottings* (1887), reports that four Grenadiers hauled into the hall a 172-pound royal baron of beef. It was draped in the Union Jack and installed under a portrait of Lord Nelson before being whittled to a frazzle and devoured.

•

The pronunciation of **English place names** can confound even native speakers. By what murky finagling does "Worcestershire" become "Wooster"? Old Father William is baffled. A handy rhyming mnemonic for getting "Norwich" right was set down by the marvellous Mother Goose:

The man in the moon
Came down too soon
And asked his way to Norwich.
He went by the south
And burned his mouth
By eating cold plum porridge.

How to Spell It	How to Say It
Barnstaple	Barnstable
Berkshire	Barksher
Bicester	Bister
Brougham	Broom
Cholmondeley	Chumlee
Frome	Froom
Great Barugh	Great Barf
Gloucester	Gloster
Keighley	Keethlee
Leicester	Lester
Lympne	Lim
Shrewsbury	Shrowsbree
Stanton St. John	Stanton Sinjen
Tintwistle	Tinsel
Trottiscliffe	Trosslee
Woolfardisworthy	Woolzee

•

The estimable Dr. Thudicum has this to say about cold porridge and plum porridge, which, in his book, are two separate entities:

Cold Porridge is a pudding-like preparation. When this dish is made sufficiently thick, or stiff, or concentrated, it becomes solid on cool-

16

ing and standing, like the starch-jellies previously described. It may be eaten cold, with cold warm sauce, or be fried, or immersed in milk.

Plum Porridge, De la Grouté, or Sweet Porridge, is a historical dish, as it was made by the Lord Addington as Coquus Regius or Grand Queux, and presented by him to the Sovereign at the coronation banquet. Before the coronation of George IV (1820) the then Lord of Addington (Archbishop of Canterbury) claimed of the Court of Privileges that he should have the opportunity to serve this dish; the claim was granted, and the Archbishop presented the dish De la Grouté to the King. The plums in this porridge were probably, as in plum-pudding, raisins and currants.

Dr. Thudicum, a keen etymologist, also notes that

in some of the casual wards of the London workhouses the gruel given as nutriment to able-bodied paupers passes under the name of skilly, a word perhaps derived from the name of a vessel used in cooking, called skillet, perhaps from Old French escuellette, diminutive of escuelle, Fr. Écuelle, from Lat. Scutella, diminutive of scutra, a dish or plate, the word from which scullery (dishery) also is derived. Hence a scullion is a dish-washer.

Persons Partial to Porridge

Old Father William is deeply steeped in oatmeal lore of all kinds. It is my principal fuel, excellent roughage, and the reason that, on most days, I can claim a comfortable Bristol Scale 4 rating. This fondness for porridge is something else I have in common with my alter ego, Henry Welby, the hermit of Grub Street. His life and circumscribed adventures are described in Chambers's *Book of Days* (1869):

> In all the time of his retirement he never tasted fish nor flesh. He never drank either wine or strong water. His chief food was oatmeal boiled with water, which some people call gruel; and in summer, now and then, a salad of some cool, choice herbs. For dainties, or when he would feast himself, upon a high day, he would eat the yoke [sic] of a hen's egg, but no part of the white; and what bread he did eat, he cut out of the middle part of the loaf, but of the crust he never tasted; and his continual drink was four shilling beer, and no other; and now and then, when his stomack served him, he did eat some kind of suckers; and now and then drank red cow's milk, which Elizabeth fetched for him out of the fields, hot from the cow.

Admirable old Elizabeth, hobbling along the crowded, stinking streets of Shakespeare's London, as alert as her cataract-encumbered eyes would allow her to be for the flash of incarnadine hide that would signal the possibility of hot milk for the boss's gruel.

Centuries later, Browning asked, "Who fished the murex up? What porridge had John Keats?" This is one of literature's great unanswered questions, ranking alongside such posers as how do you solve a problem like Maria? And how do you thank someone who has taken you from crayons to perfume? I am reluctant to wade into the marshy terrain of Keatsian gruel, but here are a few other cullings from my files on the subject.

{ In April 2007, Alec Holden of Epsom, in Surrey, England, celebrated his one-hundredth birthday. How did he do it? Oatmeal porridge for breakfast. }

Graham Kerr

In 1997, when the U.S. Food and Drug Administration issued a document touting the health benefits of oats, this Antipodean television personality's opinion was sought and offered. The Galloping Gourmet said, "I've loved oatmeal all my life and am thrilled at this news from the FDA. I'm looking forward to a tidal wave of creativity caused by this news." Nothing about these two sentences rings true for Old Father William, who has never achieved a state of ecstasy as a consequence of an FDA announcement and who knows very well about the tidal waves oatmeal can bring on, which no one could properly call "creative." The wire service item that bore these happy tidings went on to report that Mr. Kerr began every day with oatmeal, to which he added dried cranberries, raisins, and milk, topped with honey and his "special nut and seed mixture." He must have been a miracle of regularity, and I hope that he remains so, to this very day, whatever his disposition otherwise.

Certain Centennial Celebrants

Journalists love asking newly minted centenarians how they did it, what tactics they employed to duck the scythe of the reaper. In April 2007, Alec Holden of Epsom, in Surrey, England, celebrated his one-hundredth birthday by picking up a cheque owed him for winning a bet that he would achieve centenarian status. How did he do it? Oatmeal porridge for breakfast, he said. In 2005, Sidney Platt had made the same claim on reaching that landmark birthday, in London. He was enrolled at the time in a computer course and boasted of having flown a plane at the age of ninety-two, which is perhaps not word that one would want leaked to aviation authorities.

Captain James Cook

His journal for October 28, 1769, notes that his crew was keeping busy making brooms from some South Sea bushes that were suited for just such a purpose. The sailors were also harvesting a kind of native celery that he was having steamed up with their morning oatmeal, which food he calls "a great antiscorbutick." I have no idea what that means, but I love saying it.

Dr. Pye Henry Chavasse

A little better than a hundred years later—no doubt certain members of Cook's oatmeal-eating crew were still extant and gumming their way through bowl after bowl of the boss's great antiscorbutick—the doctor's groundbreaking, if rather stern, *Advice to a Mother on the Management of Her Children and the Treatment on the Moment of Some of Their More Pressing Illnesses and Accidents* (1878) instructed his readers that

> when a child has costive bowels, there is nothing better for his breakfast than well-made and well-boiled oatmeal stir-about, which ought to be eaten with milk fresh from the cow. Scotch children scarcely take anything else, and a finer race is not in existence; and, as for physic, many of them do not even know either the taste or the smell of it! You will find Robinson's Pure Scotch Oatmeal (sold in packets) to be very pure, and sweet, and good. Stir-about is truly said to be "the halesome parritch, chief of Scotia's food."

Dr. Chavasse owes a debt to Burns for the quote, and might well have been in the pay of the Robinson's company. Who's to know?

Eloise

It's possible that many youngsters in the last century were inculcated with the health-giving attributes of gruel by the author Kay Thompson, who famously put porridge in the mouth of her young heroine, a resident at the Plaza, along with these words: "You have to eat oatmeal or you'll dry up. Everybody knows that."

Robert Louis Stevenson

In *Virginibus Puerisque,* he offers evidence that playing with one's food—at least when that food is oatmeal—can sometimes pave the way to great things:

> When my cousin and I took our porridge of a morning, we had a device to enliven the course of the meal. He ate his with sugar, and explained it to be a country continually buried under snow. I took mine with milk, and explained it to be a country suffering gradual inundation. You can imagine us exchanging bulletins; how here was an island still unsubmerged, here a valley not yet covered with snow; what inventions were made; how his population lived in cabins on perches and travelled on stilts, and how mine was always in boats; how the interest grew furious, as the last corner of safe ground was cut off on all sides and grew smaller every moment; and how in fine, the food was of altogether secondary importance, and might even have been nauseous, so long as we seasoned it with these dreams.

RLS and His Cousin Devour Their Treasured Islands

Instructions for better living

HOW TO GET POTABLE WATER
WHILE LOST AT SEA IN A SMALL BOAT

The condenser was made from three tomato cans. The first had a cover, and was used as a container in which to boil water. The second can contained cold water to condense the steam. These were connected by a tube which was made from a third tomato can in this fashion: A strip of tin about an inch wide was cut, round and round the can, similar to a long, continuous strip of skin pared from an apple. The strip was then rolled, spirally, into a tube of sufficient length, about one-quarter or three-eighths of an inch in diameter. This tube was fitted into a hole made in the first tomato can, and passed through the second can, in which two holes had been made. The end of the tube projected from the second can, and beneath it was placed a bottle to catch the drops of fresh water as they fell one by one from the mouth of the tube.

The tube was wound with cloth or marlin, and the joins where the tube passed through the tin cans were made tight. The entire apparatus was fastened to the thwart of the boat.

The tin cover of Mrs. MacArthur's trunk was used for a fireplace, and for fuel the oars, planking, "ribbons," thwarts and gunwales of the boat were used—every part that could be sacrificed without weakening the structure of the boat.

The captain's wife said later, "We used to sit and count the drops, as the condensed water dripped into the bottle."

—John Grove, ed., *The Desert Island Adventure Book:*
True Tales of Famous Castaways Told by Themselves (1933)

An Outside Line

I should add a brief further word here about Jane Nurse, who entered Old Father William's orbit as a Meals on Wheels volunteer, and has become, in a way, his conduit to the roiling universe beyond Dude Cottage's smallest room. In ways that are, as it turns out, quite literal, she is a lifeline.

I have never been one to implement a high-tech solution, or to engage in activities that require the use of anything other than the simplest of the simple tools. One of my rules in life is that if it can't be fixed with duct tape, it stays broken. My last negotiation with the outside world, before I took my retreat, was to rig up a clothesline, a kind of umbilical arrangement for the conveyance of nourishment into the womb where I nestle. It runs from the locked gate of the high fence, traverses the little garden—by now, a tangled testament to whatever nature has in mind—and enters the house through the ever-open window, which also allows the cats entrance and egress. I laid in a modest supply of sturdy clothespins and a few Ziploc bags, sufficiently sized to accommodate dinner for one. Miss Nurse signals her arrival by ringing the handbell she carries about with her, a curious bit of baggage—perhaps she also uses it for self-defence, should the need arise. I send the bags out empty, and she sends them back full. It's a tidy arrangement.

Ziploc bag   +   notes   +   clothespegs   =   link to the outside world

Quite early on in our relationship—if so scary and contemporary a word can be applied to the situation—we began to exchange notes.

"What's new?" she might ask, prosaically.

By way of response, I might clip to the line, say, my little list of porridge eaters.

On her next visit she might reply, as indeed she did,

J

Dear Old Father William,

Perhaps your list of oatmeal eaters could include Mr. Woodhouse, the hypochondriacal father to the eponymous Emma in Jane Austen's novel. His recommendation for whatever ails one is "a basin of gruel." At least, that is how I remember it. Also, you might be interested to learn, if you don't know already, about Martin Ramirez (1895–1963), an artist and schizophrenic who was confined to the DeWitt State Hospital in northern California and who mixed his own colours from a paste made of such ingredients as fruit juice, mashed crayons, charcoal, and spit. He would smoosh all this up in a bowl of his own manufacture: it was sculpted out of oatmeal and dried on top of the radiator. Just thought you might like to know.

J.N.

Travelling Companions

Captain Cuttle's instruction "When found, make a note of" is, as I've said, one to which I try to adhere. Every so often, however, I'll find a little square of tissue on which I've scribbled some snippet and, carelessly, failed to include attribution. I am puzzling over one now. It says, in handwriting that is incontestably mine, "Björk, when she's on the road, cooks her own porridge every morning in her hotel room. She also travels with five suitcases, in which she carries her favourite books and vases."

It annoys me more than I can say that I failed to record where I found this arcane morsel. Find it I surely did; my imagination is neither so fertile nor so febrile that I could invent biographical or dietetic facts pertaining to mono-monikered Icelandic pop stars. Darling Björk. Imagine, possessing a sensibility so refined that one couldn't bear to be separated from one's favourite vases. Here at Dude Cottage, should a vase be required, it would have to be an old Folgers coffee tin, and then I'd have to empty it of the chicken schmaltz. Does Björk travel with her favourite vases in order to have a place to put her favourite flowers? And if so, what are they? Some other totems, animate and not, packed by persons of note to bring them comfort or remind them of home.

Swan Feather Dress, better than bubble wrap for vases

Champagne

According to H.L. Wesseling in *Divide and Rule: The Partition of Africa, 1880–1914*, **Henry Morton Stanley**—as in, "Dr. Livingstone, I presume"—always travelled with champagne, as well as a folding bed and a silver service. Also, **Matvei Ivanovich Platov** (1751–1818), the general who commanded the Don Cossacks during the Napoleonic wars, was fond of Shampanskoye, a Cossack wine *fait à la méthode champenoise,* from the Tsimlanskoi neighbourhood. He always travelled with barrels of the stuff.

Blood

A more prosaic requirement of another general. French president **Charles de Gaulle**, worried about assassination attempts and possible transfusion requirements, travelled with a bag of his own blood. Robert and Isabelle Tombs, in their book about Anglo–French relations, *That Sweet Enemy,* tell the story of M. le Président showing up for dinner one night at 10 Downing Street, when Harold Macmillan was in residence. Instructed by the visitor's bodyguards to put the bag of blood in the fridge, the cook declined, explaining that it was too full of haddock.

Mustard

Louis XI always travelled with his own supply of mustard, according to Barry Levenson, curator of the Mount Horeb Mustard Museum, Mount Horeb, Wisconsin. And Barry should know.

Chocolatier

What is with these people, the French I mean, and their inability to uproot without the assurance of familiar food to be had between points A and B? Louis had the mustard pot, and in 1638, **Cardinal Mazarin** engaged an Italian chocolate maker with whom he always travelled; likewise, a little more than a century later, **Marie Antoinette** reserved a space for such a position in her entourage.

Asses

Mind you, Marie Antoinette, who washed her face in red wine to forestall the arrival of wrinkles—one wants a smooth complexion when one's head is held up to the jeering masses—couldn't hold a cosmetic candle to **Poppea**, wife of Nero, who is said to have travelled everywhere with five hundred nursing asses, so that she could take an asses' milk bath whenever she felt the need. Old Father William has always found that a tin of condensed cow juice smeared liberally around with a coarse, exfoliatory cloth and worked into the crevices with a cotton swab also works very well.

Ukulele

George Harrison always travelled with two, one for him and one for somebody else who might like to play.

Metronome

When items from Maria Callas's estate came up for auction in 2007, her metronome was among the chattels. According to the Sotheby's catalogue, it accompanied the celebrated soprano on all her travels.

Grandma Moses

Cole Porter was a fan of Grandma M. and made hotel rooms more homey by hanging a small painting of hers. A *New York Times* reporter wrote in 1948, "Cole Porter is a trim, slight man, groomed with subdued, elegant taste. The only bright touch in his get-up when he was visited a few days ago in his apartment on the forty-first floor of the Waldorf Towers was a white carnation. The most colorful thing in the room was a big painting by Grandma Moses, full of her naively gay whites and blues, which hung in a place of honor over the piano."

Parrots

Samuel Butler, in his essay "Ramblings in Cheapside," wrote, "I met a lady one year in Switzerland who had some parrots that always traveled with her and were the idols of her life. These parrots would not let anyone read aloud in their presence, unless they heard their own names introduced from time to time. If these were freely interpolated into the text they would remain as still as stones, for they thought the reading was about themselves. If it was not about them it could not be allowed." (See also *Polly Math.*)

Books

Henry James Sr., father of Henry and William and Alice, and author of *The Secret of Swedenborg*, never travelled without bringing along the works of his avatar, Emanuel Swedenborg, which would have required a sizable trunk if he took the complete oeuvre.

Henry Elkins Widener, for whom the Widener Library at Harvard is named, and who died on the *Titanic*, was an avid collector of Robert Louis Stevenson and never travelled without his copy of *Treasure Island*, which he is said to have known by heart.

Alec Guinness never went on a journey of any distance without an Anthony Trollope novel. (No doubt there are novel trollops who never go on a journey of any distance without a pint of Guinness, but Old Father William has never heard of them.)

Stuffed Owl

Florence Nightingale rescued an owlet from some boys who were torturing it and carried everywhere in her pocket. It died shortly before she went to Crimea and she delayed her departure so that it could be stuffed.

Tennis Ball

Bert Bobbsey, as revealed in *The Bobbsey Twins at the Seashore*:

The afternoon was wearing out now, and the strong summer sun shrunk into thin strips through the trees, while the train dashed along....

"Won't we soon be there?" asked Freddie, for long journeys are always tiresome, especially to a little boy accustomed to many changes in the day's play.

"One hour more," said Mr. Bobbsey, consulting his watch.

"Let's have a game of ball, Nan?" suggested Bert, who never traveled without a tennis ball in his pocket.

"How could we?" the sister inquired.

"Easily," said Bert. "We'll make up a new kind of game. We will start in the middle of the car, at the two center seats, and each move a seat away at every catch. Then, whoever misses first must go back to center again, and the one that gets to the end first, wins."

"All right," agreed Nan, who always enjoyed her twin brother's games. "We will call it Railroad Tennis."

Just as soon as Nan and Bert took their places, the other passengers became very much interested. There is such a monotony on trains that the sports the Bobbseys introduced were welcome indeed.

Teddy Bear

English poet and broadcaster **John Betjeman**, from very early on and throughout his entire life, travelled with his bear, Archie—full name, Archibald

The American Express slogan, "Don't Leave Home Without It," was launched in 1975.

Ormsby-Gore—and his stuffed elephant, Jumbo. Betjeman took the bear to Oxford, and he and Archie became the models for Sebastian Flyte and Aloysius, respectively, in Evelyn Waugh's *Brideshead Revisited.*

Donald Campbell, the speed record setter on both land and water, always travelled with his lucky bear, Mr. Woppit, named for a line of bears produced by the Merrythought company. "Woppit" morphed to "Whoppit," and news agencies around the world reported how, in January 1967, Campbell climbed into the cockpit of his Bluebird hydroplane, clutching Mr. Whoppit and with a water speed record of 300 mph in view. He had reached a velocity of 340 mph when the boat reared up, flipped over, and broke in two. *Time* magazine (January 13, 1967) reported that Campbell had been playing solitaire on the night before his record attempt and "turned up the ace and queen of spades in succession. 'Mary Queen of Scots had the same combination before she was beheaded,' he remarked. 'I know that one of my family is going to get the chop. I pray to God it isn't me.'" Mr. Whoppit was found floating among the debris, but Campbell's body was not recovered until 2001.

Stuffed Chimpanzee

Primatologist **Jane Goodall** always travels with a stuffed chimpanzee named Mr. H. She still has, she has told interviewers, Jubilee, the stuffed chimp her father gave her when she was a very young child.

Wet Bar

Mohandas Gandhi travelled everywhere with his goat, a tool of self-rule whose milk helped stave off the need for the purchase of English products and was healthy, to boot. In *Time* magazine (November 2, 1931), we read,

> Before he left Bombay for London, St. Gandhi protested loud and long that he expected nothing whatever to come of the Indian Round Table Conference. Last week while the conference, hopelessly hung up on the problem of Hindu-Moslem representation, still struggled on, he quietly booked passage to sail back to India the middle of November.
>
> Meanwhile in the English Dairy Show at the Royal Agricultural Hall the benign nanny goat that provides Mahatma Gandhi with his goat's milk defeated all comers in her class, had a blue ribbon hung about her scrawny neck and was officially named "Mahatma." Chief concrete result of the human Mahatma's visit is that in London the price of goats and goat's milk has gone up. At Kingsley Hall, where St. Gandhi sleeps and spins, a secretary disclosed that during the first days of his visit goat's milk was hard to get and cost about four shillings ($1) a pint, could be found only in wholesale apothecary shops dealing in roots, herbs and obscure drugs.

MAHATMA!

Gandhi's Dandy Nanny

We'll Meet Again—Not!

On September 23, 1931, **Mohandas Gandhi** was in London and so was **Charles Chaplin**. They met, for the first and only time. Did they talk of goats? Perhaps. History is littered with such one-and-only meetings.

•

On August 27, 1965—the very date that **Bob Dylan** was booed off the stage in Forest Hills, New York, the **Beatles** and **Elvis** had their only meeting, on the opposite coast, in Bel Air, California. The Beatles knew Dylan by then, sort of. They had their one meeting towards the end of their U.S. tour in 1964. In her book *Wonderful Tonight,* Pattie Boyd, once married to George Harrison, tells the story of how Dylan, listening to "I Want to Hold Your Hand," had misconstrued the line "I can't hide" as "I get high," and came to the Fab Four's hotel room bearing a joint, and not of beef.

•

If **Sigmund Freud** had heard Dylan sing "Forever Young," might he have understood the lyric as "Forever Jung"? Freud never had the chance to hang with Bob Dylan, sad to tell, but he did have a single collision with **Gustav Mahler**. They met in August 1910, in Leyden, Holland, at Mahler's instigation, and spent four hours together walking and talking. Mahler told the father of psychoanalysis the story of how, as a child, he fled the house to escape a quarrel between his parents, ran into the street, and there encountered a hurdy-gurdy player cranking out the folk song "Ach, du lieber Augustin." From that moment on, deep tragedy and light amusement had an easy meeting in his mind. Freud took this all in, made note of Mahler's Holy Mary fixation, and then they got on their separate trains and went their separate ways.

•

In May 1922, James Joyce threw the asthmatic Marcel Proust for a loop when he lit up in a taxi.

In the same year, Mahler also had his one meeting with **Thomas Mann**, who distilled the composer's essence and siphoned it into the character of Aschenbach in *Death in Venice*. Many years later, **Susan Sontag**, aged fourteen and fresh from reading *The Magic Mountain*, tracked Mann down in Pacific Palisades and had tea with him: it was their only meeting, and Sontag complained that he "talked like a book review."

•

Did Freud, after his chat with Mahler, settle himself into his train compartment and light up one of his famous cigars? And if so, was it merely a cigar? On the occasion of their only meeting, at a late supper in Paris in May 1922, **James Joyce** wound up sharing a cab with **Marcel Proust**. Joyce threw the asthmatic Marcel for a loop when he lit up in the taxi.

•

Ernest Hemingway, who was friendly with Joyce in Paris, didn't smoke cigarettes—he told Lillian Ross in the *New Yorker* that they interfered with his sense of smell, which got in the way of his hunting—but surely he joined **Fidel Castro** in sucking back a celebratory cigar on the occasion of their one meeting, on May 15, 1960, when Castro won the marlin-fishing tournament that Hemingway had sponsored at Barlovento since 1951.

•

Two Vienna-born philosophers, **Karl Popper** and **Ludwig Wittgenstein**, brandished not lighters but, apparently, red-hot pokers when they met for the first and only time in Cambridge, on October 25, 1946, and fell immediately into a violent disagreement about the existence of any moral principle.

•

Ralph Waldo Emerson's single meeting with Mary Ann Evans was rather more peaceable. About ten years before Miss Evans found wide fame as **George Eliot**, they were guests in the same house when he was lecturing in Coventry. They discovered a mutual passion for Rousseau, but she took him to task, gently, over something he'd written in one of his essays. Presumably, this is not what he had in mind when he wrote, in *The Conduct of Life,* "be willing to go to Coventry sometimes, and let the populace bestow on you their coldest contempts."

•

The meeting between **Ethel Merman** and **Igor Stravinsky** was downright cordial. L. Arnold Weissberger, in his book *Famous Faces,* reports that when they were introduced at a party in New York City in 1962, Stravinsky said, "I have long been an admirer of yours," and Merman answered, "I like your music, too." Did she "la-la" through a few measures of *The Rite of Spring* to prove the point? Did Igor sing a rousing chorus of "I Got Rhythm?" Old Father William regrets more than anything that he couldn't have been a fly on the wall for that one.

•

In 1819, through the agency of a mutual friend, **John Keats** and **Samuel Taylor Coleridge** met for the only time, a chance encounter while out walking. Keats described the encounter, and Coleridge's wide-ranging conversation, in a letter to his brother:

> In those two Miles he broached a thousand things—let me see if I can give you a list—Nightingales, Poetry—on Poetical Sensation—Metaphysics— Different genera and species of Dreams—Nightmare—a dream accompa-

{ **When Ethel Merman met Igor Stravinsky in 1962, she said to the composer, "I like your music, too."** }

nied with a sense of touch—single and double touch—a dream related—First and second consciousness—the difference explained between will and Volition—so say metaphysicians from a want of smoking the second consciousness—Monsters—the Kraken—Mermaids—Southey believes in them—Southey's belief too much diluted—a Ghost story—Good morning—I heard his voice as he came towards me—I heard it as he moved away—I had heard it all the interval—if it may be called so. He was civil enough to ask me to call on him at Highgate.

What a Grecian Earns Is Owed to a Nightingale

Coleridge and Keats spoke of nightingales, about which bird each had written or was to write. Chambers's *Book of Days* describes the work of a Jesuit named **Marco Bettini** who, in the sixteenth century, syllabized nightingale song in this way:

Tiouou, tiouou, tiouou, tiouou,
Shpe tiou tokoua;
Tio, tio, tio, tio,
Konoutio, konoutiou, konotiou, koutioutio,
Tokuo, tskouo, tskouo, tskouo,
Tsii, tsii, tsii, tsii, tsii, tsii, tsii, tsii, tsii, tsii, tsii,
Kouorror, tiou, tksona, pipitksouis,
Tso, tso, tso, tso, tso, tso, tso, tso, tso, tso, tso, tso,
tsirrhading.
Tsi, tsi, si, tosi, si, si, si, si, si, si, si, si,
Tsorre, tsorre, tsorre, tsorreki;
Tsatu, tsatu, tsatu, tsatu, tsatu, tsatu, tsatu, tsi,
Dlo, dlo, dlo, dla, dlo, dlo, dlo, dlo, dlo,
Kouiou, trrrrrrrrritzt,
Lu, ht, lu, ly, ly, ly.

•

Enrico Caruso loved songbirds, as noted in a list laid out by his wife, Dorothy, of thirty-eight true things about her legendary husband. The complete list appears in her book *Enrico Caruso: His Life and Death* (1945).

1. Enrico was five feet nine inches tall and weighed 175 pounds.
2. His complexion was cream, without color in the cheeks.
3. He could not run well because of the formation of the Achilles tendon.
4. He took two baths a day.

5. He bathed his face with witch hazel.

6. He did not use face powder except on the stage.

7. He used Caron perfumes; he walked around the apartment with a large atomizer, spraying the rooms with scent.

8. He weighed three pounds less after each performance.

9. He did not lie down to rest during the day.

10. He did not ride, play golf or tennis, go for long walks, or do setting-up exercises in the morning.

11. He never ate five plates of spaghetti for lunch!! His lunch was vegetable soup with the meat of chicken left in, and a green salad.

12. When he was to sing, he ate only the white meat of chicken or two small lamb chops.

13. He ate the crust of bread with every meal.

14. His favorite vegetable was raw fennel, which he ate like fruit.

15. He did not eat candies or chocolate.

16. He smoked two packages of Egyptian cigarettes a day, always in a holder.

17. He would have no caged birds at the Villa in Signa.

18. He would not permit songbirds to be shot on his property.

19. He never shattered either a mirror or a wineglass with his voice, as has been stated.

20. When he was well he went to bed at midnight and slept eight hours.

21. He took no medicines of any kind except, the night before he sang, half a bottle of "Henri's Powdered Magnesia" in water.

22. He never employed a claque, although he was warmly attached to old Schol, chief-of-claque at the Metropolitan.

23. He always retained his Italian citizenship.

24. He never learned to drive a car.

Diverse Non-Drivers

Here are some others who, like Caruso, belong to the small but select fraternity/sorority of auto shunners. Old Father William, who has never even qualified for a poetic licence, not even at the learner's level, thinks that many more people than is now the case should just say no to jalopies. The piloting of several tonnes of metal into which has been siphoned a volatile fuel is nothing to take lightly.

Albert Einstein

One supposes that he was just too taken up with the pulse of the time-space continuum to deal with stick shifts and turn signals; the iconic photo of him wheeling about on a bicycle is scary enough.

Adolf Hitler

Hitler had several chauffeurs, including Erich Kempka, who was among those who oversaw the Führer's ex-bunker cremation; Julius Schreck, who died of meningitis after—according to not always reliable sources—trying to repair his own abscessed tooth with a screwdriver and hammer; and Emil Maurice, who was sacked for his romantic interest in Geli Raubal, Hitler's niece, with whom the Führer was also infatuated.

Elizabeth Bishop

The American poet with the Nova Scotia lineage and the Brazilian connection revealed this information about herself in an interview in the *Paris Review* (Summer 1981).

Wallace Stevens

The poet preferred to walk the couple of miles to his office, matching the words in his head to the beat of his feet on the pavement.

Edmund Wilson

The pre-eminent literary critic was once seen passing through Massachusetts in a taxi with a D.C. plate. (It was Wilson who drew Vladimir Nabokov's attention to a passing reference in Havelock Ellis's *Studies in the Psychology of Sex* about a man who had had encounters with nymphets and child prostitutes who were more experienced than he. A few years later, *Lolita* was born. Wilson didn't like it.)

Vladimir Nabokov

He would write while his wife, Vera, handled things at the wheel.

Eugene O'Neill

The O'Neills relied on their "man of all work," Herbert Freeman, to drive them around. (See also *Died in a Hotel*.)

Kingsley Amis

Zachary Leader, in his biography of Amis, says that K.A. never learned to drive because it would interfere with his drinking.

Evelyn Waugh

Likewise, never went to revisit Brideshead, or any other place, behind the wheel of a car.

> The English comedian Benny Hill called Anthony Burgess "the greatest living expert on sex."

Anthony Burgess

Owned but did not drive a Bedford Dormobile, a camper van, which his wife drove while he remained aft, writing at a built-in desk.

Benny Hill

The English comedian called Anthony Burgess "the greatest living expert on sex," and Burgess was among Hill's eulogizers when he died in 1992. No funny stories were told about his driving adventures. He never learned.

Robert Ripley

Believe it or not, he never drove, but did collect cars. (He was also fearful of the telephone, thinking it might electrocute him.)

John Entwistle

The Who's bassist (see *Died in a Hotel*) was another car collector who never drove.

Ava Gardner

Her non-driving status was disclosed in a post-mortem appreciation by Reid Buckley in the *National Review* (April 16, 1990).

Alfred Hitchcock

He reasoned that if he never drove he would never be ticketed by the police— at least, not for a driving infraction.

J

Dear Old Father William,

I hope you like turkey; the drumstick and cranberry sauce are in honour of Thanksgiving. I've had a very pleasant week going through a hundred boxes of foundling books: some unknown reader packed them up and left them, neatly piled, on the library's stoop. Anonymity doesn't usually feature in such large donations, and there's not a single book plate or envelope or utility bill page marker to indicate who it might have been. I've been checking them against the catalogue to determine which are required and which are de trop.

Pursuant to your list of things that people never left home without, I thought you might be interested in The Great Secret, Dr. Claude Gubler's tell-all book about his boss, the late French president François Mitterand; there are already a dozen copies in the system, and no one seems to be clamouring for more. You'll

J

note that he describes how Mitterand was thrilled by the pillows he found on his bed at one stop on a long trip: "He looked like a child amazed by an unexpected gift. He wanted me to measure the pillows and inquire about their fabrication in order to have them duplicated in Paris. Finally, to simplify the problem, I stole one pillow which I slid into the presidential luggage. The sample was given to the Élysée Palace linen keeper, who had several duplicate pillows made. François Mitterrand never traveled without them."

For your information, and happy Thanksgiving. Remember to say grace!

J.N.

P.S.: I attach my card.

JANE NURSE, BA, MLS

FREELANCE LIBRARIAN
AND DEACCESSIONING SPECIALIST

First they read it, then I weed it.

A Pillow Book for Jane Nurse

How rare to have gobbler and Gubler in the same delivery. I recall reading that **Zubin Mehta**, the India-born conductor, kept drumsticks under his pillow as a child: not legs wrested from poultry but batons used for percussive purposes. (But perhaps you understood that.) Old Father William, more prosaically, places his dentures under his pillow each and every night, in the hope that the Tooth Fairy might come along and slip him a twenty. So far, no luck. I wonder if Tooth Fairies are more cautious latterly than was once the case? They would have reason to be anxious about reaching under strangers' pillows, considering what might be there. For example, **Vicki Childress** garnered much media attention of a wry sort when, on October 21, 1991, she reached under her pillow for her inhaler, pulled out her charged and combustible .38, and shot herself through the jaw. She survived, but might have had to redraft her relationship agreement with taffy.

Quite how she could be sufficiently at ease as to sleep with a gun next to her temple is a mystery to me. Nonetheless, history both recent and well worn suggests that this is a common protocol. Among those unperturbed by so potentially problematic a proximity as a pistol packed under a pillow was the melodically named **Kinshishi Adams**—a police officer, apparently with work/home separation issues—whose .40-calibre service revolver accidentally discharged in bed and did considerable damage to her wrist, in Albany, Georgia, on June 11, 2007. Investigators reported that she was "alone at the time of the shooting." That's a relief.

Whether they're feathers or whether they're foam,
Pillows are prominent all through the home.
Pillows have cases well-fitted to sheath them,
Let's see whose treasures were buried beneath them.

W.H. Auden

In an interview in the *Paris Review,* Elizabeth Bishop says she believed Auden kept a revolver under his pillow when he was at Oxford. Did he? Or was she thinking of Audie Murphy, the American war hero and film star who, suffering from post-traumatic shock, said he always slept with a firearm under his pillow?

Robert Baden-Powell

In his charming panegyric to the founder of the Boy Scout movement, *The Story of Baden-Powell, the Wolf That Never Sleeps,* Harold Begbie writes,

> Once, after two months of wandering, he got into a hotel and, after dinner, into a bed. But it would not do, he says; in a twinkling he had whipped the blankets off the bed and was lying outside on mother earth, with the rain beating upon his face, and deep in refreshing slumber. The best of beds, according to B.-P., is "the veldt tempered with a blanket and a sad-dle." When he is on his lonely wanderings he always sleeps with his pistol under the "pillow" and the lanyard round his neck. However soundly he sleeps, if any one comes within ten yards of him, tread he never so softly, Baden-Powell wakes up without fail, and with a brain cleared for action.

Robert Blake

The star of the television series *Baretta,* who stood trial for the murder of his wife, the ten-times-married Bonny Bakley, kept his childhood cap gun under his pillow; kept it there as an adult, that is.

Judith Campbell Exner

The memoirist, who was simultaneously the paramour of both President Kennedy and Chicago mob boss Sam Giancana, claimed to have arranged business meetings between the two men at which she was present. When her affairs with these gentlemen ended, round about the same time, she began to sleep with a large dog at her bedside and a pistol under her pillow, just in case there was residual annoyance from either party; probably a prudent course of action, all things considered.

Peter Lawford

The Rat Pack principal was also, of course, the brother-in-law of J.F.K., and pistols under pillows figure among his biographical details. In his biography, *Peter Lawford: The Man Who Kept the Secrets,* James Spada writes that Lawford's mother was so discomfited by the business of heaving her son from her loins that she reached under a pillow, extracted her husband's service revolver from its resting place, and would have put an end to her painful contractions there and then were it not for the intervention of a quick-thinking attendant.

Lawford and Patricia Kennedy's son, Christopher, describes in his memoir, *Symptoms of Withdrawal,* how his childhood friend Rick Hilton showed him the revolver his—i.e., Hilton's—father kept under his pillow. Rick Hilton, some years later, would sire a daughter, Paris.

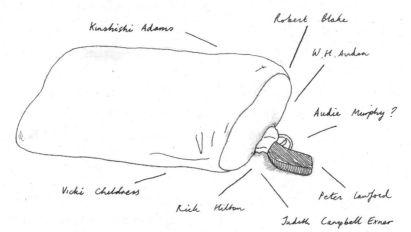

Kinshishi Adams

Robert Blake

W. H. Auden

Audie Murphy ?

Vicki Childress

Rick Hilton

Peter Lawford

Judith Campbell Exner

Vyacheslav Molotov

Generally reliable sources report that when the man who lent his name to that most exuberant of cocktails visited the White House in 1942, he kept a you-know-what you-know-where.

Alexander the Great

His biographers are fond of saying that he kept a copy of Homer's *Iliad* under his pillow, as though it were available to him in a compact Penguin Classics version. But this kind of habit would have required eventual chiropractic intervention to deal with the consequent neck bend. Legend has it that Alexander also kept a dagger alongside the *Iliad,* which raises the dire prospect of what might happen if he wanted one and reached for the other. Of course, Alexander lived long before he could profit from the example of Vicki Childress (above).

Theodore Roosevelt

He died in his sleep on January 6, 1919, in bed and with a book under his pillow; or so various insiders report, though not with sufficient specificity. What was the book? Did no one note the title? Someone must have done so, but I have looked and looked and can find no trace. Old Father William will give a prize to the first person to fill him in.

Mary Shelley

After Roosevelt's son Quentin died in the Great War, the family arranged for a stone marker inscribed, "He has outsoared the shadow of our night." The phrase is from "Adonais," Percy Shelley's elegy for Keats. The story is told that when Shelley's drowned body was cremated on the beach near Rome by Lord Byron, Edward Trelawny, and Leigh Hunt, his heart withstood the flames. An indecorous tug-of-war for ownership of the fire-resistant ticker ensued between Hunt and Mary Shelley. Mary finally won, and kept it under her pillow, wrapped in a copy of "Adonais." (So the story goes. Old Father William has his doubts. Years ago, for reasons I'd rather not disclose, I fell asleep with a slab of liver under my pillow, and even after a single night it was most unpleasant in the morning. The charms of a slightly charred heart, however well wrapped, would wear thin quite quickly, I'm certain.)

Plato

Plato's single commonality with Theodore Roosevelt—unless he was fond of hanging big game trophies all over the walls of his cave—may be that he is also said to have died with a book under his pillow. But again one wonders, what book? And what did a book look like in the time of Plato? What did a pillow, come to that? Tablets on tablets, one supposes. Whatever the format of the text,

> The best way of dealing with mimes would be a pillow held firmly over the face.

it has at least been identified, plentifully if not consistently. Some sources say it was the verses of Sappho, others say *Lysistrata,* and others still claim Plato was resting his head on the *Mimes* of Sophron, which calls disconcertingly to mind creatures in whiteface pretending to be caught behind plates of glass. Old Father William has always thought that the best way of dealing with mimes would be a pillow held firmly over the face; at least they would scream silently.

Charlemagne

He was a latecomer to literacy but keen on self-improvement, and kept writing tablets under his pillow so that he could practise his handwriting when he woke at night and had no other way to occupy his time. Of course, that was long, long before pornography on DVD.

Vladimir Nabokov

Rather more economically, he had a stash of index cards under his pillow, the better to make notes of his inspirations when he sat bolt upright in bed: "Note to self: a man with a surname the same as his first—Humphrey, Humboldt, Humbert, something like that—falls inappropriately in love with—what? A dog? A goat? A pubescent nymph? Something to explore when more awake...."

Euan Uglow

One of Mr. Uglow's life models, with whom he'd had an affair—apparently not an unusual circumstance—told the *Guardian's* Christopher Woodward (December 16, 2006) that the English figurative painter, who died in 2000, kept under his pillow a copy of Stendhal's *Charterhouse of Parma.*

Luther Evans

Evans, the librarian of Congress from 1945 to 1953, had a passion for repatriation and returned a number of manuscripts to their countries of origin. In her introduction to a recent edition of *Alice in Wonderland*—pivotal in the life of Old Father William, for sure—Zadie Smith describes the circuitous journey of the copy of Carroll that once belonged to the eponymous Alice Liddell. In 1928, strapped for cash and very old, she sold her very own Ur-text at Sotheby's. Thereafter it moved from hand to hand and country to country, winding up in America. In 1948, a consortium of Alice-o-philes decided it should be repatriated. They purchased the book for a great deal more than the original sale price. It fell to Mr. Evans to take it back to those green and pleasant lands whence it sprang, which he did on a ship, sleeping at night with the treasure under his pillow. Ms. Smith records that the Archbishop of Canterbury accepted the book on behalf of the nation and "called the gift an 'unsullied and innocent act in a distracted and sinful world.'"

L.M. Montgomery

In 1908, after the publication of another children's classic, *Anne of Green Gables,* L.M. Montgomery received a fan letter from Mark Twain. She kept it under her pillow.

Eva Lovelace

The character played by Katharine Hepburn in *Morning Glory* keeps a letter from George Bernard Shaw under her pillow.

Fyodor Dostoevsky

Whether the Russian writer stored things under his pillow I can't say, but it's certainly a device in his fiction. In *The Brothers Karamazov,* pillows conceal three thousand rubles, nasty books, a clipping from a St. Petersburg newspaper called *Gossip,* and a French exercise book. And in *Crime and Punishment,* Raskolnikov keeps a copy of the New Testament under his pillow while in the prison camp.

The March Sisters

In *Little Women,* Louisa May Alcott provides another fictive case of scripture under the pillow:

> Jo was the first to wake in the gray dawn of Christmas morning. No stockings hung at the fireplace, and for a moment she felt as much disappointed as she did long ago, when her little sock fell down because it was crammed so full of goodies. Then she remembered her mother's promise and, slipping her hand under her pillow, drew out a little crimson-covered book. She knew it very well, for it was that beautiful old story of the best life ever lived, and Jo felt that it was a true guidebook for any pilgrim going on a long journey. She woke Meg with a "Merry Christmas," and bade her see what was under her pillow. A green-covered book appeared, with the same picture inside, and a few words written by their mother, which made their one present very precious in their eyes. Presently Beth and Amy woke to rummage and find their little books also, one dove-colored, the other blue, and all sat looking at and talking about them, while the east grew rosy with the coming day.

Jane Goodall

When she who travels with a stuffed chimpanzee was a toddler, she was found to be keeping earthworms under her pillow. Much hilarity ensued in the family, as you might imagine.

James I

Apparently, he kept under his pillow the sermons of Lancelot Andrewes, the Bishop of Winchester, also the overseer of the King James version of the Bible.

The Good Book Gone Bad

In 2007, the trustees of the Victoria Public Library, in a money-making mood, sent to Sotheby's an item that had long been in their keeping: a very rare King James Bible, a so-called "He edition," one of only fifty in the world, and so named because of a bit of gender confusion. In this edition, chapter 3, verse 5 of the Book of Ruth states, "and *he* said unto her, All that thou sayest unto me I will do." "*She* said," of course, is required. Several other editions of the Bible owe their nicknames either to typographical errors or to whimsical translation:

- In the **Breeches Bible** (1560) Adam and Eve make themselves "breeches" rather than "aprons" to disguise their newly discovered nakedness.
- The **Bugge Bible** (1551) has David saying, in Psalm 91:5, "so that thou shalt not need to be afrayed for any bugges at night." The King James translation set the new—but less etymologically and entomologically interesting—standard by replacing "bugges" with "terrors."
- In the **Camels Bible** (1823), Rebekah arises in Genesis 24:61 with her "camels" rather than her "damsels."
- In the **Denial Bible** (1792), it's Philip, not Peter, who denies the Lord in Luke 22:34.
- The **Ears to Ears Bible** (1807) renders "who hath ears to hear" in Matthew 13:43 as "who hath ears to ears."
- The **Fool's Bible** (circa 1630) slips up in Psalm 14:1, advising, "The fool hath said in his heart, There is a God." "No God" is what the psalmist had in mind.
- And from 1631, we have the most blush-making example of them all, the **Wicked Bible**, which omits a small but pivotal word from Exodus 20:14. "Thou *shalt* commit adultery," says the seventh commandment in this edition, which must have made for some fascinating domestic arrangements among the pious and observant.

{ **The Wicked Bible, from 1631, reads, "Thou shalt commit adultery."** }

Come Sit for a Spell

Speaking of misprints, an article from *Time* magazine (June 6, 1937) describes the spelling bee victory in the annual Scripps contest—Scripps Howard as it was then, I believe—of Waneeta Beckley. Miss Beckley buried a field of sixteen finalists, looking on with stern and pitiless gaze as the other junior eggheads were mowed down by a relentless rain of bullets, each one inscribed with their particular names and with such orthographic oddities as georgette, meringue, gudgeon, and olfactory. Finally, only three aspirants remained. Angelo Mangieri, "totally blind" and from Hoboken to boot, was taken out by "receptacle." "Tiny" Betty Grunstra threw herself on the grenade of "plebeian." Waneeta, when offered that bait, rose to it with alacrity and accuracy and then promptly secured her place in the record books—to say nothing of the commemorative plaque and the five-hundred-dollar cheque—by giving, in their correct order, all the necessary letters of "promiscuous." Promiscuous! How can one's heart not break into at least two pieces on reading such news? Had she but waited a year she might have returned to Louisville and Holy Name School and rounded out her high school career as the good girl who nailed "sanitarium." Bad enough that she had to demonstrate her prowess with so dubious a word, but to also be described, in the pages of *Time* magazine no less, as "chunky, 14-year old Waneeta Beckley"? The grief. The humiliation.

One wonders about the lasting effects of such a glorious and public victory when it is visited on one so young. Might it have lingering consequences that are social, professional, or even medical? When Michael Kerpan Jr. won the bee in 1965, or when Molly Dieveney took the crown in 1982, with "eczema" and "psoriasis," respectively, did psychosomatic forces kick in and doom them to a future of oozing, peeling, and itching? Did Jacques Bailly's skill with "elucubrate" grease his path with unwanted midnight oil? Who can bear to consider what lurked in the wings for Stephanie Petit when she, haltingly but correctly, marshalled the components of "staphylococci?"

{ **The winning word in the 1937 Scripps Spelling Bee was "promiscuous."** }

Winning Words from the Scripps Spelling Bee

1925	gladiolus	1926	cerise	1927	luxuriance
1928	albumen	1929	asceticism	1930	fracas
1931	foulard	1932	knack	1933	torsion
1934	deteriorating	1935	intelligible	1936	interning
1937	promiscuous	1938	sanitarium	1939	canonical
1940	therapy	1941	initials	1942	sacrilegious
1946	semaphore	1947	chlorophyll	1948	psychiatry
1949	dulcimer	1950	meticulosity	1951	insouciant
1952	vignette	1953	soubrette	1954	transept
1955	crustaceology	1956	condominium	1957	schappe
1958	syllepsis	1959	catamaran	1960	eudaemonic
1961	smaragdine	1962	esquamulose	1963	equipage
1964	sycophant	1965	eczema	1966	ratoon
1967	chihuahua	1968	abalone	1969	interlocutory
1970	croissant	1971	shalloon	1972	macerate
1973	vouchsafe	1974	hydrophyte	1975	incisor
1976	narcolepsy	1977	cambist	1978	deification
1979	maculature	1980	elucubrate	1981	sarcophagus
1982	psoriasis	1983	Purim	1984	luge
1985	milieu	1986	odontalgia	1987	staphylococci
1988	elegiacal	1989	spoliator	1990	fibranne
1991	antipyretic	1992	lyceum	1993	kamikaze
1994	antediluvian	1995	xanthosis	1996	vivisepulture
1997	euonym	1998	chiaroscurist	1999	logorrhea
2000	demarche	2001	succedaneum	2002	prospicience
2003	pococurante	2004	autochthonous	2005	appoggiatura
2006	Ursprache	2007	serrefine	2008	guerdon

Interviewed by *Time* after her 1937 triumph, Waneeta Beckley, still not apprehending, perhaps, the full import of what it would mean to her to have so trippingly hauled that winning word from her brain and mouth, confessed that the hardest word for her, the one that most nearly threw her, was "baste." Quite what that signifies is far too arcane for me to grasp. Some things, I am sure, are simply better left unspelled.

Einstein was a bad speller and **F. Scott Fitzgerald** was a bad speller and so was **Andrew Jackson**, to whom some attribute the fathering of the casual affirmative "OK": shorthand for "Oll Korrect," as he approvingly wrote on state documents. "Ocian in view," wrote **William Clark** of the Lewis and Clark expedition when nearing the Pacific, thus laying bare his breast to the whetted blade of ridicule wielded by generations of pedants. In 1992, Vice President **Dan Quayle** gave a famous public demonstration of bad spelling when he amended, on an elementary school chalkboard in Trenton, New Jersey, "potato" to "potatoe": a malignant tuber, if ever there was one.

The press had a field day, as they did in 1906 when **Theodore Roosevelt**, a prolific writer (see A Pillow Book for Jane Nurse), proposed a system of spelling reforms that would apply to all government documents. This innovation did not win the hearts and minds of the nation, and it's perhaps most interesting as an insight into governmental priorities: why were these three hundred words adjudged sufficiently important, governmentally, to be weighed and found wanting and in need of adjustment? Why, in the world of federal documentation, should "artizan" replace artisan, "bark" barque, "coquet" coquette, "Eolian" Aeolian, "fagot" faggot, "nipt" nipped, or "rime" rhyme? How often, in the world of bureaucratic reportage, is one required to spell "lachrymal," or "lacrimal" in the reformed world? In the end, doesn't it all just seem a tad dum?

J

Dear Old Father William,

A busy week of deaccessioning has produced the attached little didactic volume, evidently intended for the betterment of bobbies in Edwardian London. Is it of any use to you in your enterprise? By the way, I am including a box of raisins for you—they might liven the oatmeal—and a sachet of catnip for, who else, the cats. Do they like that kind of thing?

J.N.

Jane Nurse is the most kindly of women. She has no way of knowing that Dude Cottage is a kind of rehab facility for cats with nip issues. However, they enjoyed the raisins, and Old Father William found the herb quite a spicy addition to his bath, which was where he enjoyed leafing through *Self Education for the Police*, 11th edition, distributed by Police Review Publishing. It contains the following list of "Difficult Words from Examination Papers":

adjourn	exhibit	opossum	sojourn
ambition	exhibition	phalanx	stricture
ambitious	ignite	phrase	thyme
bivouac	ignition	poignant	tonsil
comparative	kerosene	pomegranate	varicose
coquette	lobe	pregnant	verdigris
etiquette	moiety	roulette	whelk

SELF-EDUCATION

FOR

THE POLICE

FIRST COMPILED BY
H. CHILDS, F.R.Hist.S.

REVISED BY
J. RILEY, B.Sc. (Lond.)

11th Edition   55th Thousand
Price 1/6

LONDON : " POLICE REVIEW " PUBLISHING CO. LTD.
5–6, RED LION SQUARE, W.C.1

"You are old," said the youth, "as I mentioned before,
  And have grown most uncommonly fat;
  Yet you turned a back-somersault in at the door—
  Pray, what is the reason of that?"

"In my youth," said the sage, as he shook his grey locks,
  "I kept all my limbs very supple
  By the use of this ointment—one shilling a box—
  Allow me to sell you a couple?"

J

Dear Old Father William,

Any use for this first edition of Emily Post?
It would be quite valuable, I think, were
it not for evidence of somebody's long-ago
coffee spillage. How rude! By the way,
why Dude Cottage?

J.N.

Some Thoughts on the Well-Christened Domicile

J ane Nurse wonders, I suppose, as others have, if "Dude Cottage" is a coy reference to dude ranch, or if I'm clinging inappropriately to the things of youth by affecting the vernacular of mid-1990s striplings. In fact, the house was built—cobbled together would better describe it—by a gentleman named Mr. Gainsborough Dude; this was back in the days when Queen Victoria still ruled a great deal of the earth. Why Dude Cottage as opposed to the more baronial-sounding Gainsborough House is a question I can't answer. The fact is that it has always been known, hereabouts, as Dude Cottage, and I've given no thought to rewriting neighbourhood history. I am in very good company.

Consider that **Ian Fleming**'s estate in Jamaica was called Goldeneye. **Noel Coward** rented the house from him in 1948 and decided to set up his own establishment, eventually settling in the house he named Firefly.

The year 1948 also marked the twenty-fifth anniversary of his long estrangement from **Edith Sitwell**, who, along with her brothers Osbert and Sacheverell, claimed Renishaw, near Sheffield, as their ancestral seat. Sitwell and Coward feuded for thirty-five years. They were at odds over the way he parodied Edith and the family firm in his 1923 revue *London Calling*: the Sitwells were the models for his "Swiss Family Whittlebot."

Coward also took a satiric jab at **Vita Sackville-West**, who lived at Sissinghurst with her husband, **Harold Nicolson**. Somewhere along the way, Coward called her "Lady Chatterley above the waist and the gamekeeper below."

Lady Chatterley's peripatetic creator, **D.H. Lawrence**, during his time in Australia, lived in Thirroul, New South Wales, in a house called Wyewourk at 3 Craig Street. It's generally thought that Lawrence's inspiration for the randy Lady Chatterley, with her penchant for a bit of rough trade on the side, was **Ottoline Morrell**, who had an affair with Tiger, a young stonemason whose assignment on the books was to carve plinths for her garden at Garsington Manor.

Lady Chatterley's Lover and the lesbian testament *The Well of Loneliness* were among the most controversial novels of the twentieth century. **Radclyffe Hall**, author of *The Well of Loneliness*, lived in Highfield House and then in

White Cottage, both in Malvern Wells. The eccentric writer and composer and gadabout **Lord Berners**, who wrote a girls' boarding school *jeu d'esprit* called *The Girls of Radclyffe Hall,* lived at Faringdon.

Edith Wharton, whose estate in Lennox, Massachusetts, was called The Mount, wrote to **Mary Berenson** that "the dull twaddle of Miss Radclyffe Hall has to be boosted by the censors! It's a good world after all." (The letter is quoted by Hermione Lee in her biography *Edith Wharton;* she also wrote a fine biography of Virginia Woolf.)

Mary and her husband, the art critic and collector **Bernard Berenson**, lived in Fiesole, Italy, in Villa I Tatti. Mary Berenson's daughter Ray married Oliver Strachey, who was the brother of the biographer **Lytton Strachey**, who lived at Hamspray House. Ray's sister, Karin, was married to Adrian Stephen, who was **Virginia Woolf**'s brother.

Virginia and **Leonard Woolf** lived at Monk's House, in East Sussex. In her introduction to *Orlando,* which is dedicated to Vita Sackville-West, Virginia Woolf thanks Osbert Sitwell, Lord Berners, Lytton Strachey, Ottoline Morrell, and Harold Nicolson, as well as **E.M. Forster**, whose house in Hertfordshire was Rook Nest.

Woolf and Forster were among those mentioned in the so-called Black Book: a list compiled by the Nazis of persons to be captured and disposed of on the occasion of England's invasion. Also on the list were **George Bernard Shaw**, who applied the principle of eponymy to his house, Shaw's Corner, and **Robert Baden-Powell**, the founder of the Boy Scout movement; he lived at Pax Hill. Noel Coward was also in the Black Book, but ranked rather low, at ninety-three.

Coward listed among his influences **Lewis Carroll**, whose house was The Chestnuts, and **Beatrix Potter**, who lived at Hill Top, although as a child she spent her summer at Camfield Place, which became the estate of the hugely prolific romance novelist **Barbara Cartland**.

Barbara Cartland was step-grandmother to **Princess Diana**, who is buried on the Spencer family estate, and Barbara Cartland is, likewise, buried at Camfield Place, under a tree allegedly planted by Elizabeth I. The Finnish composer **Jean Sibelius** is also buried on his estate, Ainola, not so far from

Helsinki, and the charred remains of the great Norwegian composer **Edvard Grieg** were committed to the cliffside of his estate, Troldhaugen.

Peggy Guggenheim is also interred, in ash form, in the garden of her Palazzo Venier dei Leoni in Venice, now the Guggenheim Museum, alongside her dogs, whose names are inscribed thus on a marker in the Palazzo courtyard: Cappucino [sic], Pegeen, Peacock, Toro, Foglia, Madam Butterfly, Baby, Emily, White Angel, Sir Herbert, Sable, Gypsy, Hong Kong, and Cellida. It seems odd that she would give one of her dogs—Lhasa Apsos—the same name as her daughter—Pegeen—and unfortunate that "Cappucino" was misspelled, but then again, no one is or was perfect.

The only person who ever came close was the gentleman who is buried at Firefly, Mr. Noel Coward. This, at least, is how he is regarded at Dude Cottage, the home and the hermitage and, possibly, the eventual burial place of Old Father William.

have pictures of owners on reverse?

have pictures of house on reverse?

coasters.

NOEL COWARD.

ten towels ↑

Possible Money-making Schemes

Instructions for better living

How to Sit Gracefully

Having shaken hands with the hostess, the visitor, whether a lady or a gentleman, looks about quietly, without hurry, for a convenient chair to sit down upon, or drop into. To sit gracefully one should not perch stiffly on the edge of a straight chair, nor sprawl at length in an easy one. The perfect position is one that is easy, but dignified. In other days, no lady of dignity ever crossed her knees, held her hands on her hips, or twisted herself sideways, or even leaned back in her chair! To-day all these things are done; and the only etiquette left is on the subject of how not to exaggerate them. No lady should cross her knees so that her skirts go up to or above them; neither should her foot be thrust out so that her toes are at knee level. An arm a-kimbo is not a graceful attitude, nor is a twisted spine! Everyone, of course, leans against a chair back, except in a box at the opera and in a ballroom, but a lady should never throw herself almost at full length in a reclining chair or on a wide sofa when she is out in public. Neither does a gentleman in paying a formal visit sit on the middle of his backbone with one ankle supported on the other knee, and both as high as his head.

The proper way for a lady to sit is in the center of her chair, or slightly sideways in the corner of a sofa. She may lean back, of course, and easily; her hands relaxed in her lap, her knees together, or if crossed, her foot must not be thrust forward so as to leave a space between the heel and her other ankle. On informal occasions she can lean back in an easy chair with her hands on the arms. In a ball dress a lady of distinction never leans back in a chair; one can not picture a beautiful and high-bred woman, wearing a tiara and other ballroom jewels, leaning against anything. This is, however, not so much a rule of etiquette as a question of beauty and fitness.

A gentleman, also on very formal occasions, should sit in the center of his chair; but unless it is a deep lounging one, he always leans against the back and puts a hand or an elbow on its arms.

—Emily Post, *Etiquette in Society, in Business, in Politics and at Home* (1922)

Old Father William thanks Jane Nurse for this copy of Emily Post's classic guide to good behaviour. According to the inscription, it was presented to Judith Sanders of Chicago, on the occasion of her sixteenth birthday in 1924. It was not Judith, I am reasonably sure, whatever her flapper aspirations, who took a pencil and bolstered with an "h" the word "sit" in the title phrase of this section. No doubt the book made a number of stops between the Chicago of 1924 and its here-and-now roost. I suspect a child somewhere along the way, in a devil-may-care moment, made the sophomoric amendment, thrilled to think of some future grown-up's shock and horror. Certainly, it was not a monosyllable Mrs. Post would ever, ever, in a million years, have let slip from her lips, not that she was opposed to vernacular. She wrote,

> Coarse or profane slang is beside the mark, but "flivver," "taxi," the "movies," "deadly" (meaning dull), "feeling fit," "feeling blue," "grafter," a "fake," "grouch," "hunch" and "right o!" are typical of words that it would make our spoken language stilted to exclude. All colloquial expressions are little foxes that spoil the grapes of perfect diction, but they are very little foxes; it is the false elegance of stupid pretentiousness that is an annihilating blight which destroys root and vine.

J

Dear Old Father William,

It's payback time. I wonder if you might have, among your quaint and curious volumes of forgotten lore, a copy of a book I loved as a child, Napoleon's Book of Fate. It was in my grandmother's bookcase, and kept on quite a high shelf, out of the reach of childish hands. I suppose she must have imagined it would pollute our tiny minds. I can't think why she might have thought so, but evidently, she did. Altitudinous storage didn't keep us from it, of course, it just excited our interest the more: the allure of the transgressive and so on. Whenever we would visit, my sister and I would teeter atop a chair and take it down.

I recall that it contained a kind of method for divination that I was never able to grasp, and that there were also some curious lists, including one that had to do with moles—I'm

J

talking about eruptions on the skin, not the lawn. It was a kind of catalogue of what they signified, depending on where on the body they were found. I hadn't thought of this in years, but a new mole has recently set up camp on my left shoulder. I will, of course, be consulting the dermatologist about this, but would like to know if old Napoleon—or whoever is the author of said tome—has anything to say about it first.

J.N.

Moles:
Their Signification, Either in Men or Women

These significant marks of the body are very remarkable guides either to the good or bad fortunes of anyone.

- A mole on the left side of a man denotes danger and strangling; in a woman, sorrow, and great pain in childbirth.
- A mole on the left cheek foretells fruitfulness in either sex, as does one on the nose.
- A mole on the upper lip shows happiness in marriage.
- A mole on the breast shows affection loyalty, strength, and courage, which will gain honour.
- A mole on the navel shows many children to a woman; and in a man that he shall be vigorous.
- A mole in the midst of the forehead shows wisdom and conduct in the management of affairs.
- A mole on the right cheek shows the party too much beloved, and will come unto great fortune.
- A mole on the left shoulder shows sorrow and labour.
- A mole on the throat denotes the party a great glutton, and by excess will undergo a great disease and peradventure, sudden death.

NOT THE KIND OF MOLE
OF INTEREST TO NAPOLEON

- A mole on the right eye shows loss of sight.
- A mole on the forehead of a man or woman denotes they shall grow rich, being beloved of their friends and neighbours.
- A mole on the eyebrows shows the men incontinent, and given to women; but if a woman, it shows she will have a good husband.
- A mole on the nose shows that the party loves pleasure more than anything else.
- A mole on the neck shows a man to be prudent in his actions; but a woman of weak judgment, apt to believe the worst of her husband.

NAPOLEON'S
BOOK OF FATE
AND ORACULUM

CONTAINING

DREAMS AND THEIR INTERPRETATION
WEATHER OMENS: ASTROLOGICAL MISCELLANY
AND IMPORTANT ADVICE

CHIROMANCY OR FORTUNE TELLING BY THE
HAND. CELESTIAL PALMISTRY

OBSERVATIONS ON MOLES IN MEN AND WOMEN.

TEMPER AND DISPOSITION OF ANY PERSON
THE ART OF FACE READING
LUCKY DAYS, ETC., ETC.

London
W. FOULSHAM & CO., LIMITED
10 & 11, Red Lion Court, Fleet Street, E.C 4.

How to Make a Leech Barometer

Take an eight-ounce phial and three-parts fill it with water, and place in it a healthy leech, changing the water in summer once a week, and in winter once in a fortnight, and it will most accurately prognosticate the weather. If the weather is to be fine, the leech lies motionless at the bottom of the glass, and coiled together in a spiral form; if rain may be expected, it will creep up to the top of its lodgings, and remain there till the weather is settled; if we are to have wind, it will move through its habitation with amazing swiftness, and seldom goes to rest till it begins to blow hard; if a remarkable storm of thunder and rain is to succeed, it will lodge for some days before almost continually out of the water, and discover great uneasiness in violent throes and convulsive-like motions; in frost as in clear summer-like weather it lies constantly at the bottom; and in snow as in rainy weather it pitches its dwelling in the very mouth of the phial. The top should be covered over with a piece of muslin.

—*Enquire Within upon Everything* (1894)

A leech Barometer

fine — coiled

Rain

Wind

Storm

frost — coiled

Snow

Tabled for Your Consideration

Old Father William had just such a barometer for many years. It worked very well until the gizmo's active ingredient did the mortal coil shuffle. I found the pale creature on the kitchen table one morning, bearing on its person the unmistakable marks of cat interference. It was a sad day at Dude Cottage: feeding the leech was a ritual I quite enjoyed, and I liked knowing that my blood was being used in the service of predicting weather patterns. There's a stain on the table where Leechy perished; I considered having it removed, but decided to leave it as a kind of memorial to a life well lived. It's rather more usual for life to begin on a kitchen table, as the following demonstrates. Sort of.

•

On June 10, 1921, the future **Prince Philip**, Duke of Edinburgh, was born on the kitchen table of the Villa Mon Repos, in Corfu. His father was Prince of Greece and Denmark, his mother a granddaughter of Queen Victoria. Presumably there was a very nice cloth involved and the forceps, if required, were sterling. Perhaps the attending obstetrician availed himself of nearby sugar tongs.

•

Edna Staebler was born on January 15, 1906, in what was then Berlin, Ontario. The name was changed to Kitchener in 1916. "Kitchen" figured large in her life. She became a hugely popular cookbook author, which seemed foreordained given that she, like Prince Philip, had her advent on the kitchen table. She died in 2006, a few months after receiving her congratulatory hundredth-birthday telegram from the Prince's wife.

•

On May 26, 1938, soprano **Teresa Stratas**, like Prince Philip of Greek descent, was born in Toronto, above a Chinese restaurant at the corner of Dundas and George Streets, on, legend has it, her parents' dining room table. That was the very day, Ascension Thursday, that Adolf Hitler laid the cornerstone for

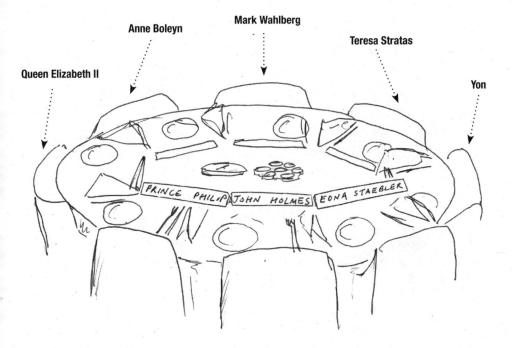

Queen Elizabeth II

Anne Boleyn

Mark Wahlberg

Teresa Stratas

Yon

PRINCE PHILIP | JOHN HOLMES | EONA STAEBLER

Table Laid for Company with Knives, Spoons, Forks, and Forceps

a Volkswagen plant in Fallersleben, Lower Saxony. Popular legend has it that Hitler was testicularly short changed: one of the regulation two, according to some historians of such anomalies, failed to descend. Film star and former underwear model Mark Wahlberg, on the other hand, has a supernumerary endowment: he was born with three nipples. They aren't credited but can be seen quite plainly by anyone with the patience to watch the 2007 conspiracy theory epic *The Shooter*.

•

Anne Boleyn's peculiar paw: the reason why she never hitchhiked?

On August 8, 1944—a Tuesday—**John Holmes** was born on a kitchen table in Ashville, Pickaway County, Ohio. His endowment was his fortune; he was possessed of a member of staggering dimensions: fourteen inches, or so he claimed. It was not a taper he hid under a bushel—or a pillow, come to that. He showed the thing off in hundreds of films of dubious worth before he died, of AIDS, in 1988. Mark Wahlberg portrayed a fictionalized version of Holmes in the 1997 film *Boogie Nights*. Like Mark Wahlberg, Anne Boleyn was said to have had three nipples, as well as a sixth finger. Anne Boleyn was the mother of Elizabeth I, who, through her aunt Margaret Tudor, passed on the royal line to Elizabeth II, who married her third cousin Prince Philip of Greece and Denmark, who was born on a kitchen table.

J

Dear Old Father William,

Good news on the dermal front. The mole was nothing but a mole. The word "benign" is a pretty one when you've been girding your loins for the other. By the by, I found these three equations noted in my grandson's history notebook. What do they represent? Any clue?

1. $Q_{in} = (\mathcal{E}_A/C_A)(e^{2\,(PA-PC)/\mathcal{E}A} - 1)$
2. $Q_{out} = (\mathcal{E}_V/C_V)(1 - e^{2(PV-PC)/\mathcal{E}V})$
3. $P_C = a_1 \ln(a_2 V_C) + a_3 e^{a_2 VC}$,

where Q represents arterial pressure,
$\mathcal{E}$ represents arterial elasticity,
A represents artery, V represents vein,
P_C represents corporeal pressure,
and P_V represents corporeal volume

J.N.

Dear Jane Nurse,

Quite how I know what this is, I'd rather not disclose: it's a mathematical model describing the erectile mechanism of the penis. You must sit down immediately and have a chat with the lad. Why is he keeping his biology notes in his history book? This must stop. It can't happen a moment too soon.

For your interest, I append the following extract from a book that was given to me by my own father, many, many years ago, a sex education manual called As You Become a Man, by Raymond V. Arntfield. It was self-published in 1938, a paperbound volume that has the look of having been run off on the mimeograph in the church basement. How Papa acquired it I have no idea: plainly it was a very limited run. Perhaps it arrived in the mail in a plain brown wrapper. In the mode of Lord Chesterfield, the book consists of letters written to a son. They explain the physical changes that accompany adolescence, and the desires that overtake a boy as he enters his years of maturation.

Predictably, there are anti-masturbatory adumbrations. This is Mr. Arntfield's list of reasons why boys must avoid this destructive habit. Is this information you would like to pass on to your grandson? I expect not, somehow.

O.F.W.

FIRST

Because obviously, God expected that a human being would have enough sense to leave his sex parts alone. Outside of apes, man is the only male animal which has been given arms and hands long enough to reach his sex organs. No other animal CAN play with itself. MAN is expected to have enough sense NOT TO WANT TO DO IT.

SECOND

The loss of sperm and semen should be avoided because these substances are the VERY FLUID OF LIFE and a great deal of energy and strength go into their making. The loss of these substances, except in a natural way, when the storage ducts are full, is to be carefully avoided.

THIRD

Your conscience will tell you that self-abuse is WRONG.

FOURTH

Such a practice is extremely hard on the nervous system and CAN produce insanity IF CARRIED TO EXTREMES.

FIFTH

The coarse treatments thus given the very sensitive sex parts will toughen them and may finally make them incapable of carrying out the great purpose for which they were created.

J

Dear O.F.W.,

I think I'll pass on the Arntfield
and let the lad get up to whatever
it is he gets up to, out in the
woodshed.

J.N.

Shedding Season

It's Ada Doom, in *Cold Comfort Farm,* who sees something nasty in the woodshed. Much can be witnessed in such outbuildings, if one happens to peep in at just the right time.

Motorcycles

In 1903, in Milwaukee, **Bill Harley** and the **Davidson** boys, Art and Walt, got together in the shed behind the Davidson family home. What they had in mind was messing around with a motor and a bicycle. The three-horsepower machine that evolved from their tinkering was the progenitor of the line of motorcycles that bears their names. Would their fortunes have been different had they decided to call their invention the "Davidson-Harley"? We'll never know.

By way of noting how these things can play out, consider that on Valentine's Day, 2008, at the Crazy Horse Saloon in Paris, Pamela Anderson paid tribute to fellow bombshell Brigitte Bardot by performing a striptease to Bardot's hit song "Harley Davidson." It was meant to have something to do with her campaign against the seal hunt. Old Father William seems to recall that the French word for seal is "phoque," which somehow seems germane, though I'm not sure why.

Jazz

Harley and Davidson pioneered the chopper, and jazz great **Charlie Parker**—the story is perhaps apocryphal—improved his chops in a woodshed. That's where he practised as a young musician, taking quite

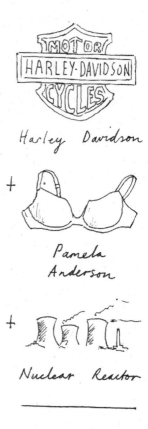

Harley Davidson

+

Pamela Anderson

+

Nuclear Reactor

shed

literally, or perhaps coining, the term "woodshed-ding." Kerouac alludes to this in *On the Road*: "Charlie Parker, a kid in his mother's woodshed in Kansas City, blowing his taped-up alto among the logs, practicing on rainy days, coming out to watch the old swinging Basie and Benny Moten band that had Hot Lips Page and the rest."

Aluminum

In an Oberlin, Ohio, woodshed in 1886, **Charles Martin Hall**, then twenty-two, conducted the experiments that led eventually to the production of aluminum. Mr. Hall filed twenty-two U.S. patents. He neither married nor spawned, so far as anyone knows, and funnelled much of his money, of which there was a great deal, to Oberlin College. There he is memorialized by a statue made of, what else, aluminum. It was highly portable and was, for many years, ported by collegians on a spree to fanciful locations round about the campus. Now, Mr. Hall's likeness is adhered to a granite block and not subject to removal.

Airplanes

Aluminum gave a certain lift to the work of other celebrated Ohioans, the **Wright brothers**, who were inveterate shed putterers while growing up on Hawthorn Street, in Dayton. Geeks long before the word was coined, they got up to all sorts of research-based shenanigans out back where the wood got chopped and the rakes got hung and the flies died and dried on the sills. They set up a darkroom to develop photographic plates, and, of course, they began their anti-gravitational theorizing, which led, over time, to their shed in Kitty Hawk and then, inexorably, to mass airborne migration, enhanced security systems, and the widespread implementation of the cavity search (see *Namesake Specula*).

Frozen Corpses

Frozen Dead Guy Days is a celebration enjoyed each March by the residents of Nederland, Colorado. It features coffin races, a parade that takes place in very slow motion, and frozen dead guy look-alike contests. This is all in the name of feting the presence in town of a frozen Norwegian, **Bredo Morstøl**, whose remains are consigned to a Tuff shed. Mr. Morstøl died in Norway in 1989, and was imported into the United States post-mortem by his grandson, Trygve Bauge. After the frozen stiff had spent some considerable time in *very* cold storage, in a cryogenics facility, Mr. Bauge and his mother (i.e., Bredo's daughter), Aud, decided to bring him closer to home: they set up a cryogenics facility in the backyard. Complications, some involving immigration, ensued. Word got out. Consternation was expressed. Then everyone decided it was better to make hay while the Norse froze. Mr. Morstøl's name was moved from the liability side of the ledger to the asset side, and Frozen Dead Guy Days was born. Anyone who thinks the United States of America is an empire in decline will surely reassess that notion on hearing of this adjustment. A Colorado-based confectionery, Glacier Ice Cream, turns out a seasonal delight called Frozen Dead Guy. A highly granular and otherwise textured affair, it consists of gummy worm, Oreo cookie crumbs, and a lot of blue colorant added to fruity ice cream. Incidentally, Peters Ice Cream, a gelato purveyor of Antipodean prominence, was engendered in an Australian backyard shed.

More Metals

Stef Wertheimer, the Israeli billionaire industrialist and centrist politician, founded Iscar Metalworking in a backyard shed in 1952. In 2006, Warren Buffett acquired a majority share of the company for five billion dollars. Old Father William would like it communicated to Mr. Buffett that he is available for acquisition for a mere fraction of that price.

Nuclear Reactors

David Hahn, a Boy Scout with a special interest in the radioactive, manufactured a small nuclear reactor in a backyard shed in suburban Detroit, in 1994. Authorities became involved. Promises were extracted. Recidivism settled in. In 2007, he brushed up against the law again, this time for stealing smoke detectors, presumably with some kind of illicit manufacture in mind. He was sentenced to ninety days.

Gin

Bols Jenever, gin by any other name in any other place than Holland, was first brewed in a riverside shed near Amsterdam in 1595. The family's pet name for the distillery, "'t Lootsje," translates to something like "the little shed." Old Father William wishes he were better schooled in Dutch, just as he wishes he were less phlegmish.

Pornography

Dutch courage might have been required by **Sharon Thomas**, a forty-one-year-old Welsh housewife whose neighbours had no cause to believe that she used her shed for anything other than the storage of daffodil bulbs and the drying of leeks. In fact, her tiny outbuilding was the epicentre of a smallish porn empire, from which she distributed salacious catalogues to customers worldwide.

Sex

Mrs. Thomas might have cited, in defence of her use of the shed, the precedent of *Lady Chatterley's Lover*. In that landmark novel, it's in the shed that clothes are shed:

> The hut was quite cosy, panelled with unvarnished deal, having a little rustic table and stool beside her chair, and a carpenter's bench, then a big box, tools, new boards, nails; and many things hung from pegs: axe,

> David Hahn, a boy scout, manufactured a small nuclear reactor in his backyard shed in suburban Detroit in 1994.

hatchet, traps, things in sacks, his coat. It had no window, the light came in through the open door. It was a jumble. But also, it was a sort of little sanctuary....

He laid his hand on her shoulder, and softly, gently, it began to travel down the curve of her back, blindly, with a blind stroking motion, to the curve of her crouching loins. And there his hand softly, softly, stroked the curve of her flank, in the blind instinctive caress.

And so on.

Also of literary note is the woodshed where the baby who may be the salvation of the world is conceived in P.D. James's dystopian novel *The Children of Men*.

Shelter

It was in the De Lacey family's woodshed that **Dr. Frankenstein's monster** took shelter and, there concealed, observed the family's ways and learned English. Roald Dahl, the English author of such children's classics as *Charlie and the Chocolate Factory* and *James and the Giant Peach,* and, by every reliable account, a most unpleasant man, did much of his writing squirrelled away in a garden shed. And, of course, it's in a woodshed that that pilfering leporine delinquent, **Peter Rabbit**, sought refuge from the vengeful Mr. McGregor.

Another young felon's woodshed hideout features in this article from the *New York Times* (December 14, 1896):

Moxie Ownski, the "king of the burglars," was caught last night, about 12 o'clock by Special Burkhardt of the Eighth Precinct, while sleeping in a woodshed at the rear of a house on Railroad Avenue.

Special Burkhardt has done some remarkable work during the last few days since his transfer took place. Last night he went out to get the Burglar King, who is the executive head of the gang that has been operating in Buffalo lately, and Burkhardt got him without much trouble. He

{ **The baby who may be the salvation of the world is conceived in a woodshed in *The Children of Men*.** }

has captured, with the help of Capt. Kress and Special Lazewski, nine of these petty thieves.

"This gang is the worst one ever organized in this part of the city," said the Doorman of the Eighth Precinct Station, "and this fellow is the leader of them all."

From the way in which Special Burkhardt spoke about this burglar chief, anyone would come to the conclusion he was quite a man, but when he was brought into the Stationhouse it was found he was nothing but a 14-year-old boy.

Dishwashers

In contrast to the foregoing, the woodshed was used for entirely salubrious purposes by **Josephine Garis Cochrane**. In the 1880s, Mrs. Cochrane—she started out as Cochran, then added the "e" to fancy things up—who was the daughter and granddaughter of inventors, had simply had enough of dishwashing. Out she went to the shed, armed with nothing more than dishpan hands and ingenuity. She re-emerged with an automated response, a primitive but effective way of loading dishes into a cage, lowering them into sudsy water, swishing them around, and then spraying them clean. She acquired a patent (No. 355139) and made her first sale to the Sherman House Hotel in Chicago. In an interview with the Chicago *Record Herald* (November 24, 1912) she said,

That was almost the hardest thing I ever did, I think, crossing the great lobby of the Sherman House alone. You cannot imagine what it was like in those days, twenty-five years ago, for a woman to cross a hotel lobby alone. I had never been anywhere without my husband or father—the lobby seemed a mile wide. I thought I should faint at every step, but I didn't—and I got an $800 order as my reward.

She exhibited her machine at the 1893 World's Fair in Chicago and won first prize for "the best mechanical construction for durability and adaptation to a particular line of work." One of the nine concessionaires who used her gizmo at the World's Fair wrote this testimonial: "On Illinois Day your machine washed without delay soiled dishes left by eight relays of a thousand soldiers each, completing each lot within 30 minutes."

God

William Branham, the Pentecostal faith healer, had his first vision round about the age of seven, when an angelic voice warned him never to drink or smoke or defile his body in any way—some sources say the visitation took place at his father's still, which may or may not have been in a shed. When he was twenty-ish, recovering from a nasty work accident and fearful of dying, he went behind the shed at his home and asked for God's intervention. According to a 1952 biography, *William Branham: A Prophet Visits South Africa*,

Suddenly there appeared a light in the form of a cross and a voice spoke to him in language he did not understand. Then it went away. He became frightened and wondered as he said, "Lord, if this is you, please come back and talk to me again." The light reentered the shed. As he prayed, it appeared again the third time. Now he realised that he had met God. He was happy; he was thankful.

Surgical Equipment

In 1998, **Dr. Steve Hindley**, a British GP working as a locum in the Australian outback near Ravensthorpe, used a rusty drill found in a school shed to drill

{ **Josephine Garis Cochrane exhibited her dishwasher at the 1893 Chicago World's Fair.** }

a hole in the left temple of a football player. Hayden McGlinn, twenty-three, had suffered a blood clot after a head-on collision with another sportsman. He recovered; Dr. Hindley and his family moved to Tasmania.

Dissection

And finally, on April 11, 1848, no fewer than eight doctors gathered in a tool shed in Bergamo, Italy, for the autopsy of **Gaetano Donizetti** (see *Died at Fifty*), the prolific composer of such bel canto operatic classics as *Lucia di Lammermoor, La fille du régiment,* and *Maria Stuarda.* Drs. Novati, Cima, Zendrini, Ronzoni, Calvetti, Cassis, Locatelli, and Maironi signed the document, which makes for invigorating reading aloud at the dinner table. Here is what they had to say about the great composer's head, according to *Donizetti,* by Herbert Weinstock:

> The integuments having been removed, a very great symmetry of the osseous parts, forming an ample and elevated dome, was revealed. The skull-vault having been sawed off all around, a diffuse venous infusion of the meninges was observed. In the hollow of the arachnoid was found a notable quantity of liquid, totaling approximately one ounce, a quantity that was increased further when the brain was lifted out; circumvolutions corresponding to the locality of the organs of music, of mentation, and of genius; the corresponding bone was thinned down until no thicker than a fingernail.

How to Recognize Musicality

A SINGER should have the Mental-Vital temperament, to give pathos and intensity. Large Tune, large Language, Eventuality, and strong moral and social organs. THE ORGANIST requires mechanical talent and a taste for combinations, to operate the instrument, and carry all the parts; he needs Combativeness, Self-esteem, Firmness, Tune, Eventuality, and Locality.

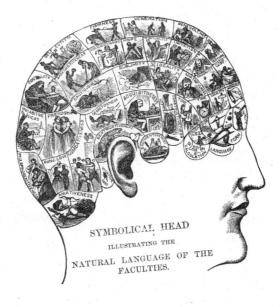

SYMBOLICAL HEAD

ILLUSTRATING THE

NATURAL LANGUAGE OF THE
FACULTIES.

—Nelson Sizer, *Heads and Faces: How to Study Them* (1887).
The different parts of the brain mentioned would be discernible to the skilled phrenologist through palpating the bumps and ridges of the skull.

For Those Who Find a Sheep's Head and Wonder How Best to Use It

In Great Britain mutton is the most generally useful form of animal food, as well on account of its intrinsic qualities as of the adaptability of its parts to the smallest and largest wants. In Scotland, where barley, thistles, and sheep thrive equally well, mutton enjoys various forms of popular preparation, which lose much by transference to other climates. The preparation of the head of the sheep for cooking there begins with singeing with a red-hot iron; if this were practised in London, it would lead to the interference of sanitary committees of vestries, perhaps of the Local Government Board itself; however, singeing completed, the horns, if any are present, are sawed off; the head is soaked in warm water and scraped. In England the head is mostly deprived of its skin, which is consequently not cooked. The head is next split, and the brain is removed; this can be made into forcemeat-balls, or be used otherwise.... Soak the head in water during the night to be able to bleach and clean it. Put it into a stewpan with water, and boil it with some vegetables.

That description I copied from Dr. Thudicum's magisterial *Cookery: Its Art and Practice*. There is much to be gained from reading it, as there is from frequent immersion in Mrs. Beeton's *Book of Household Management*. Like any great book, it sustains constant referral, and the sun glances off its myriad nuggets of wisdom at surprising times and in surprising ways. Only this morning, for instance, in the bath, I was surprised by an unanticipated sub-equatorial stirring, and when I looked down to see the cause (and effect) of it, I was reminded of Mrs. Beeton's insights into the parsnip: "In its wild state, the root is white, mucilaginous, aromatic, and sweet, with some degree of acrimony: when old, it has been known to cause vertigo." And didn't that sum up my situation to a T?

Oh, Mrs. Beeton. There has never been a time in my life when you have not been among my companions. Childless, I sometimes wonder to whom I should consign my copy, once I'm no longer among the quick. I am the third, and apparently the last, generation of my family to enjoy the very particular diversions offered by the sainted Isabella—remarkable to think that she was but twenty-eight when she died. In the pages of Isabella B., one finds, among the recipes and suggestions for organizing the parlourmaids, such snippets as this, concerning the serving of singed sheep's heads:

> The village of Dudingston, which stands "within a mile of Edinburgh town," was formerly celebrated for this ancient and homely Scottish dish. In the summer months, many opulent citizens used to resort to this place to solace themselves over singed sheep's heads, boiled or baked. The sheep fed upon the neighbouring hills were slaughtered at this village, and the carcases were sent to town; but the heads were left to be consumed in the place.

It's possible that Mrs. Beeton's competence didn't extend to spelling: "Duddingston" is the more usual rendering of the name. While the custom of sheep's head singeing—it isn't over till the fat lady singes—seems to have gone by the boards, Duddingston remains home to the Sheep's Heid Inn, putatively Scotland's oldest pub (1360). Duddingston is also memorialized in the famous Henry Raeburn painting *The Reverend Robert Walker Skating on Duddingston Loch*.

The Perils of Sheep's Clothing

In May 2003, **Malcolm Flockton**, forty-one, died in police custody after he was arrested for throwing a brick through his fiancée's former boyfriend's window. He was sporting a sheepskin at the time he committed the infraction, a costume he favoured most usually for around-the-house wear. Marijuana was apparently involved.

•

In October 2005, **Marco Schelb**, twenty-one, a German student wearing a sheep costume made of paper, cotton wool, glue, and hairspray, was accidentally set alight at a harvest festival. His four friends tried to extinguish the blaze, but they were likewise attired and likewise ignited. Mr. Schelb survived, but sustained burns to 26 percent of his body.

•

The Perils of Sheep's Clothing

In December 2004, in Birmingham, an eighteen-year-old cast as a sheep in a nativity play was set aflame and sustained 10 percent burns to his hands, lower back, and buttocks.

•

In December 2007, at a party held at the RAF base in Linton-on-Ouse, in the vicinity of York, a twenty-six-year-old trainee pilot dressed as a sheep was set on fire. He sustained 10 percent burns. The twenty-three-year-old who wielded the lighter was arrested.

•

Tim Waygood, who runs a company called Motiv-Action, and who is engaged by corporations in the United Kingdom to engender a sense of purpose and unanimity among employees, advocates an exercise called Human Sheep wherein one worker, dressed as a sheep, is herded into a pen by his or her co-workers, who can communicate only with tambourines and whistles. Old Father William is *very* glad he works alone.

A Person on Business from Porlock: A Minor Catalogue of Dreamers

ere are a few instances, some well known, some obscure, of persons who have found, on the shores of waking, useful flotsam deposited there by the waves of dreaming.

•

Madame C.J. Walker (1867–1919), who was described in her obituaries as "New York's wealthiest negress," and whom the *Guinness Book of World Records* identifies as the first self-made woman millionaire in the United States, accrued her wealth through the manufacturing and marketing of beauty products. In 1895, she was suffering from a scalp complaint and hair loss. None of the patented products she tried had a laudable effect. Then, one night, "I had a dream, and in that dream a big, black man appeared to me and told me what to mix up in my hair. Some of the remedy was grown in Africa, but I sent for it, mixed it, put it on my scalp, and in a few weeks my hair was coming in faster than it had ever fallen out. I tried it on my friends; it helped them. I made up my mind to begin to sell it." In 1917, she moved into her Italianate villa in Irvington on Hudson. Her obituary noted that it cost a quarter of a million dollars to build. It was Enrico Caruso who christened the villa Lewaro, after Madame Walker's daughter, **Le**lia **Wa**lker **Ro**binson. Also of operatic interest is *Queenie Pie*, Duke Ellington's jazz opera inspired by the life of Madame Walker. It was unfinished at the time of his death in 1974.

•

The founding father of Wyocena, Wisconsin, was **Major Elbert Dickason**. The town's name came to him in a dream of a densely populated metropolis. In said reverie, he met a stranger and asked the name of this oneiric Gotham. The stranger spelled it out: "W-I-O-C-E-N-A." And as Dickason dreamed it, and

> To dream you see a flock of sheep feeding is a very favourable omen; it denotes success in life.
> —*Napoleon's Book of Fate*

since he owned all the land on which the town was built, so it was; eventually, who knows why, the "I" was replaced with that sometimes vowel, "Y." The population of Wyocena is 668, 96.1 percent of whom are white. In 2007, one registered sex offender lived there. Tornado activity is 91 percent greater than the overall U.S. average. Major Dickason would be proud.

•

Giuseppe Tartini (1692–1770), the composer and virtuoso fiddle player, told this story to the astronomer Jérôme Lalande, who recorded it in his book *Voyage d'un français en Italie:*

> One night, in the year 1713, I dreamed that I had made a compact with the Devil, and that he stood at my command. Everything thrived according to my wish, and whatever I desired or longed for was immediately realised through the officiousness of my new vassal. A fancy seized me to give him my violin to see if he could, perchance, play some beautiful melodies for me. How surprised I was to hear a sonata, so beautiful and singular, rendered in such an intelligent and masterly manner as I had never heard before. Astonishment and rapture overcame me so completely that I swooned away. On returning to consciousness, I hastily took up my violin, hoping to be able to play at least a part of what I had heard, but in vain. The sonata I composed at that time was certainly my best, and I still call it the "Devil's Sonata," but this composition is so far beneath the one I heard in my dream, that I would have broken my violin and given up music altogether, had I been able to live without it.

•

The enigmatic phrase "Ah! böwakawa poussé, poussé," contained in the song "#9 Dream," came to **John Lennon** in a dream in which two women were calling his name along with this peculiar circumlocution. Likewise, the melody for "Yesterday" came to **Paul McCartney** in a dream in 1965. The lyric was some time insinuating itself into the mix. For the first few months of its life, the words were "Scrambled eggs, oh my darling how I love your legs." And in her liner notes to the album *Red Dirt Girl,* **Emmylou Harris** writes that her song "Michelangelo" came to her in a dream.

•

One of many reasons to travel to Florence is to see the Biblioteca Medicea Laurenziana, and to marvel at the optically arresting staircase. The architect was **Michelangelo**, and the design, with its three flights of stairs, is said to have come to him in a dream.

•

Sometimes a staircase is just a staircase, but one can't help but take into account this case study from **Sigmund Freud**'s *Interpretation of Dreams:*

> One of my patients, a man whose sexual abstinence was imposed on him by a severe neurosis, and whose (unconscious) phantasies were fixed upon his mother, had repeated dreams of going upstairs in her company. I once remarked to him that a moderate amount of masturbation would probably do him less harm than his compulsive self-restraint, and this provoked the following dream: His piano teacher reproached him for neglecting his piano playing, and for not practising Moscheles's *Études* and Clementi's *Gradus ad Parnassum.* By way of comment, he pointed out that Gradus are also steps and that the keyboard itself is a staircase, since it contains scales (ladders). It is fair to say that there is no group of ideas that is incapable of representing sexual facts and wishes.

•

Another architect whose name and reputation have survived the vagaries of time figures in this dream story, told by John Aubrey in his *Miscellanies upon Various Subjects* (1696):

> When **Sir Christopher Wren** was at Paris, about 1671, he was ill and feverish, made but little water, and had a pain in his reins [kidneys]. He sent for a physician, who advised him to be let blood, thinking he had a plurisy: but bleeding much disagreeing with his constitution, he would defer it a day longer: that night he dreamt, that he was in a place where palm-trees grew, (suppose Egypt) and that a woman in a romantic habit, reached him dates. The next day he sent for dates, which cured him of the pain of his reins. Since, I have learned that dates are an admirable medicine for the stone.

•

One hundred and twenty-five years later, **Mary Shelley** had a strange and lingering dream:

> When I placed my head upon my pillow, I did not sleep, nor could I be said to think. . . . I saw—with shut eyes, but acute mental vision—I saw the pale student of unhallowed arts kneeling beside the thing he had put together. I saw the hideous phantasm of a man stretched out, and then, on the working of some powerful engine, show signs of life, and stir with an uneasy, half-vital motion. Frightful must it be; for supremely

frightful would be the effect of any human endeavor to mock the stupendous Creator of the world.

And so was born, with almost no heaving, Frankenstein.

•

Robert Altman told the film critic Roger Ebert that his 1977 film *3 Women*, both story and casting, came to him in a dream, all in one fell swoop. He woke up, got to work, and shot the film pretty much as he had dreamed it:

•

Samuel Coleridge told a not dissimilar story about the genesis of "Kubla Khan":

In the summer of the year 1797, the Author, then in ill health, had retired to a lonely farm-house between Porlock and Linton, on the Exmoor confines of Somerset and Devonshire. In consequence of a slight indisposition, an anodyne had been prescribed, from the effects of which he fell asleep in his chair at the moment that he was reading the following sentence, or words of the same substance, in "Purchas's Pilgrimage": "Here the Kubla Khan commanded a palace to be built, and a stately garden thereunto. And thus ten miles of fertile ground were inclosed in a wall." The Author continued for about three hours in a profound sleep, at least of the external senses, during which time he has the most vivid confidence, that he could not have composed less than from two to three hundred lines; if that indeed can be called composition in which all the images rose up before him as things, with a parallel production of the correspondent expressions, without any sensation or consciousness of effort. On awaking he appeared to himself to have a distinct recollection of the whole, and taking his pen, ink, and paper instantly and eagerly wrote down the lines that are here preserved. At this moment he was unfortunately called out on business by a person from Porlock, and detained by him above an hour, and on his return to his room, found, to his no small surprise and mortification, that though he still retained some vaguer and dim recollection of the general purport of the vision, yet, with the exception of some eight or ten scattered lines and images, all the rest had passed away like the images on the surface of a stream into which a stone has been cast, but, alas! without the after restoration of the latter.

·

A variation on Coleridge's disappointment attaches to the dream of **Otto Loewi**, winner of the 1936 Nobel Prize in medicine. On Easter Sunday 1920, Loewi dreamed of the way that frog's hearts could be used to demonstrate that synaptic signalling was chemical and not electrical. He woke, wrote it all down, fell asleep again, and in the morning couldn't decipher his scribble. Luckily, the next night saw the dream's resurrection. This time he rose, went to his lab, and got to work. Sixteen years later, he was rewarded for his diligence with a trip to Stockholm.

·

Any summer traveller stuck behind a lumbering Winnebago on a long stretch of two-way road can curse the dream of trailer pioneer **Richard St. Barbe Baker**. Best known for his work as a forest conservationist, he was a student at Cambridge University when he had a dream about a motorized travel trailer. This was just after the First World War, and he used surplus plane parts—thirty-six undercarriages and plywood—to build a small fleet of prototypes. Further development and marketing proved impractical, but the damage was done and his place in the Trailer Hall of Fame was secured.

•

Hannibal said that the plan to traverse the Alps on elephants came to him in a dream. In an interview with the *New York Times* (February 9, 2006), Laurent de Brunhoff, who took over the production of the Babar books from his father, Jean de Brunhoff, said that he never dreams of elephants. In "Beliefs Common in Ceylon" (*Western Folklore,* April 1960), Gwladys Hughes Simon says that, in Sri Lanka, a dream of elephants denotes imminent honour and fame; dreaming of rings is predictive of marriage. Hannibal sent back to Carthage bushel baskets full of rings cut from the hands of fallen Roman soldiers.

•

Rings of another kind—the molecular ring construction of benzene—figured in the serpentine dream of the chemist **August Kekulé**:

There I sat and wrote my Lehrbuch, but it did not proceed well, my mind was elsewhere. I turned the chair to the fireplace and fell half asleep. Again the atoms gamboled before my eyes. Smaller groups this time kept modestly to the background. My mind's eyes, trained by visions of a similar kind, now distinguished larger formations of various shapes. Long rows, in many ways more densely joined; everything in movement, winding and turning like snakes. And look, what was that? One snake grabbed its own tail, and mockingly the shape whirled before my eyes. As if struck by lightning I awoke. This time again I spent the rest of the night working out the consequences.

•

Shostakovich, whose life had more than a few nightmarish aspects to it, was also influenced by dreams. On New Year's Eve 1926, he dreamed he was walking in a desert. An old man appeared and told him that the year ahead would be a lucky one. On waking, Shostakovich resolved to make quick work of his Second Symphony; he could hear it in his head, he said. And on August 1, 1953, he wrote to the pianist Almira Nazirova that he had received the third movement of his Tenth Symphony in a dream.

Dmitri Mendeleev dreamed the **periodic table** in 1869. The Russian geologist Alexander Alexandrovich Inostrantsev told of how he came to visit Mendeleev and found him a downcast state. Mendeleev had been burning the midnight oil, trying to find a way to express systematically what he understood intuitively, that there was an order to the elements. Finally, after several days of fruitless trying, he fell asleep and when he woke, voilà, everything fell into diagrammatic shape.

In some versions of the story, he'd been sorting through his notes on index cards, arranging them as though he were playing Patience. In others, he fell asleep listening to chamber music being played in the next room—presumably not on Classical Leningrad FM—and understood in his sleep that the connection between the elements was, essentially, a harmonic one. The musical angle, if apocryphal, has a certain appeal when one takes into account that Dmitri Shostakovich's father was a student of Mendeleev.

Less reported, but no less significant, was the invention of the periodical table, in 1927, by Bettina Judman. She was fifteen years old and working as a library page in the city of Winnipeg. When asked about her accomplishment years later, she simply shrugged and said, "We just needed some place to put those magazines."

It has often been reported in the popular press that **Jack Nicklaus** dreamed of a new way of gripping the club that vastly improved his swing. It has never been reported, as near as Old Father William can learn, whether or not Mr. Nicklaus, in his dreaming state, tried out the grip on the putter nature gave him.

J

Dear Old Father William,

I've been having a busy week in the stacks of a medical library, and thought you might be interested in this volume, long out of use: *Rest and Pain: A Course of Lectures on the Influence of Mechanical and Physiological Rest in the Treatment of Accidents and Surgical Diseases, and the Diagnostic Value of Pain,* delivered by John Hilton, Surgeon Extraordinary to Her Majesty the Queen, and published in 1879. Pay special attention to page 158, where you'll find a passage that complements, in an alarming way, your excerpt from *As You Become a Man.*

J.N.

Surgeons are often consulted regarding onanism and its treatment, and it is a very important matter. It is a habit very difficult to contend with in practice. I know of no way of preventing onanism except by freely blistering the penis, in order to make it raw, and so sore that it cannot be touched without pain. This plan of treatment is sure to cure onanism. I have adopted it during more than twenty years. Gentlemen have come to me and said, "I have for many years suffered from this abominable, disgusting habit, and I have tried to cure myself of it, but I cannot; for my morbid inclination overcomes my disgust when awake, and when asleep I think I am sometimes pursuing it. Can you offer any suggestions?"

I have said, "Paint this strong solution of iodine over the whole of the skin of the penis every night; and if that does not make the organ too sore for you to touch it, then apply in the same way a strong blistering fluid to the penis." The result in practice of my experience has been that in almost every instance the continuance of the habit has thus been entirely prevented.

LARGE.

FIG. 88.—THE GOOD BOY.

SMALL.

FIG. 89.—THE BAD BOY.

Ten Donkeys, Pinned with Tales

Rest and Pain, by the seemingly sadistic Dr. Hilton, is part of a series: *Wood's Library of Standard Medical Authors*. Grateful as I am to receive it, I must point out that, as boons go, this one is not unalloyed. Now I feel compelled to "collect them all"; to books, as to cats, Old Father William finds it difficult to say no. With books, as with cats, I sometimes regret that I came into this world with so tender a heart. It can be difficult to reconcile domestic space, which is limited, with feline and/or bibliographic supply, which is infinite. This is yet another way in which my life resembles that of my ancestor in temperament, Henry Welby, the hermit of Grub Street. Henry, in his solitude, became a kind of one-man deposit library. He arranged to receive a copy of every book published in the London of his day, although he restricted his reading to those that he knew would be morally uplifting.

From Jane Nurse I have also recently received a volume in Guy Cadogan Rothery's *House Decoration* series. *Chimneypieces and Ingle Nooks* it's called, and I had a good, long look at it this morning whilst astride the commode. As is my wont, I began reading not at the beginning but by applying the principle of random opening; the Fates who govern these things—they are distant cousins, maybe, of the minor deities who preside over what happens in Vegas and stays in Vegas—steered my parachute to a chapter devoted to chimneypieces of the Tudor period. There I read, "We are still sadly oppressed by the tyranny of the hideous 19th-century chimney pot, ugly in its nakedness, hideous when cowled." I was thrilled to find myself confined in so base a place as the bog in the company of a sensibility so burnished that it could apply the concept of tyranny to something as banal as a chimney pot.

In the middle section of this book, devoted to the Gothic period, I found a reference to a Yuletide episode described by the medieval chronicler Jean Froissart, in his account of the Hundred Years' War, thus:

On Christmas Day, when the Count de Foix was celebrating the feast with numbers of knights and squires, as is customary, the weather was piercing cold, and the count had dined, with many lords, in the hall. After dinner he rose and went into a gallery, which has a large staircase of twenty-four steps: in this gallery is a chimney where there is a fire kept when the count inhabits it, otherwise not; and the fire is never great, for he does not like it: it is not for want of blocks of wood, for Béarn is covered with wood in plenty to warm him if he had chosen it, but he has accustomed himself to a small fire. When in the gallery, he thought the fire too small, for it was freezing and the weather very sharp, and said to the knights around him: "Here is but a small fire for this weather." The Bourg d'Espaign instantly ran down stairs; for from the windows of the gallery, which looked into the court, he had seen a number of asses laden with billets of wood for the use of the house; and seizing the largest of these asses with his load, threw him over his shoulders and carried him up stairs, pushing through the crowd of knights and squires who were around the chimney, and flung ass and load with his feet upward on the dogs of the hearth, to the delight of the count and the astonishment of all.

The rudeness of it, and on Christmas, of all days. There are few feast days that ought to mandate the humane treatment of donkeys, but Christmas is surely one of them. What's more, the injury was compounded by the insult of namelessness. But then, how many donkeys can any of us name, other than the fictive few who have found fame in literature? There is Eeyore, of course, in *Winnie the Pooh,* and Rucio, Sancho Panza's mount in *Don Quixote,* and the eponymous Balthazar in the heartbreaking film *Au hasard Balthazar.* Nor should we forget the equally titular Sylvester in William Steig's celebrated "not really for children children's book," *Sylvester and the Magic Pebble.* Those creatures will live forever, but here are ten other named donkeys who inhabited the transient realm of flesh and blood and whose names might not come so readily to mind.

Yanka Doodoo

An Egyptian donkey who came to the 1893 World's Columbian Exposition in Chicago. Achmet, the donkey boy in charge, spoke to the press, who, in the

How to Kill Flies

An excellent "kill at sight" solution is made by getting a little formalin from the chemist, mixing a
spoonful of it with two spoonfuls of sugar, and adding a glass of lime water. Put this in a deep plate
and float on the surface a sheet of blotting paper.
The mortality should be sufficient to satisfy the
most discerning of persons.

—*The Second Book of Hundreds of Things a Girl Can Make* (1946)

rather insensitive manner of the day, recorded his remarks in vernacular transcription:

> My father he donka boy, his father, he donka boy, why not? Oh, yes sair; me good man. Me go to mosque fife time a day. Once, fife clock in morn; twos, seben clock in morn; threes, twel clock; seen, four clock; seen, fife clock 'gain. Oh, yes. Tank, sair. Tar-boom-de-ay. Boss danka boy. In my country plenta people ride Yanka Doodoo, best donka in Cairo, sair. Me run behind Yanka Doodoo fife hours at time. Yes, sair. Oh, yes.

Royal Gift

Royal Gift, aptly named, was a gift from the King of Spain to George Washington: a jack donkey from hardy Iberian stock. It was Royal Gift, mated with a mare whose name has sadly been forgotten, who sired the first of a line of sturdy American mules.

Modestine

This was the donkey immortalized by Robert Louis Stevenson in his charming *Travels with a Donkey in the Cévennes*. He made this twelve-day tour in the fall. Among his equipment was a kind of sleeping bag of his own design that, I note belatedly, might have found its way onto my sausage list:

> This child of my invention was nearly six feet square, exclusive of two triangular flaps to serve as a pillow by night and as the top and bottom of the sack by day. I call it "the sack," but it was never a sack by more than courtesy: only a sort

of long roll or sausage, green waterproof cart-cloth without and blue sheep's fur within. It was commodious as a valise, warm and dry for a bed. There was luxurious turning room for one; and at a pinch the thing might serve for two. I could bury myself in it up to the neck; for my head I trusted to a fur cap, with a hood to fold down over my ears and a band to pass under my nose like a respirator; and in case of heavy rain I proposed to make myself a little tent, or tentlet, with my waterproof coat, three stones, and a bent branch.

Shinto

Inspired by Stevenson, the contemporary English travel writer Tim Moore made a five-hundred-mile pilgrimage to Santiago de Compostela with a donkey named Shinto.

Abdul

Also known as Murphy and sometimes called Duffy, this was the donkey employed by Private John Simpson Kirkpatrick, also known as John Simpson, in his work as a stretcher-bearer during the battle of Gallipoli. Simpson was killed in action on May 19, 1915, shot through the heart in Monash Valley, and buried on the beach at Hell Spit. The pair are commemorated by a statue in Melbourne, and were featured on an Australian stamp in 1965.

Louis

In 1953, Louis arrived at Colby College, in Waterville, Maine, to serve as mascot to the football team, the Mules. According to the Associated Press (the name of which agency, with its preliminary "Ass," seems most apropos), Louis—who was not a mule but a Sicilian donkey—had retired from an active career in show business, having appeared on television with Gary Moore, Jackie Gleason, and Arthur Godfrey; he had also graced the stage of the Metropolitan Opera, in *Aida*. Louis lasted a year as Colby's mascot, and then was traded in for a white mule.

{ In September 2005, Juan Valdez and his donkey, Conchita, were voted "most recognizable icon." }

Spookendyke

Spookendyke, familiar to readers of the *Little House* books, was the donkey Rose Wilder Lane rode a mile to school in Mansfield, Missouri.

Conchita

The companion of the fictive Juan Valdez, the emblem of the Colombian Coffee Federation. In September 2005, during an advertising symposium in New York City, delegates voted Conchita and Juan "most recognizable icon."

Ufayr

The prophet Muhammed's donkey, who, according to legend, threw himself into a well after his master's death to prevent anyone else riding him.

Jenny

Given that any old female donkey is a jenny, there are surely many tales to tell about donkeys so named. In this case, a less salubrious version of the tale of Ufayr, a five-hundred-pound donkey named Jenny was rescued after she fell into a septic tank near San Antonio, Texas, on April 24, 2007. Edward Dugosh, one of the firefighters who came to her assistance, told reporters, "It's a nasty hole, smells terrible. It's just the worst environment imaginable."

Instructions for better living

HOW TO STAY HEALTHY YEAR ROUND

January. Let not Blood, and use no Physick, unless there be a Necessity: Eat often and avoid too much sleep.

February. Be sparing in Physick, and let not Blood without absolute Necessity, and be Carefull of catching Cold.

March. Purge and let Blood: Eat no gross Meats.

April. It is now a good Time to bleed and take Physick; abstain from much Wine, or other strong Liquors; they will cause a Ferment in your Blood, and ruin your Constitution.

May. The Blood and Humours being now in Motion, we must be careful to avoid eating Salt, strong or stale Meats; fat People must avoid Excess of Liquors of any Kind.

June. Cooling Sallads, as Lettice, Sorrel, Purslane, &c. will prevent too great a Perspiration, and throw off Feverish Disorders.

July. Forbear superfluous Drinking. Use cold Herbs. Shun boil'd, salt and strong Meats, and abstain from Physick.

August. This month use moderate Diet, forbear to sleep soon after Meat; for that brings Opilations, Headachs, Agues, and Cathars, and other Distempers of the same Kind. Take great Care of sudden Cold after Heat.

October. Avoid being out late at Nights, or in foggy Weather; for a Cold now got, may continue the whole Winter.

November. The best Physick this Month, is good Exercise, warm Clothes, and wholsome Diet: But if any Distemper afflict you, finish your Physick this Month, and so rest 'till March.

December. Keep your Feet warm by Exercise, your Head cool through Temperance, never eat till you are a hungry or drink but when Nature requires it.

—*Rider's British Merlin: For the Year of Our Lord God 1758,*
Compiled for His Country's Benefit, by Cardanus Rider.
Horticultural instructions are also given in the original.

And from the same source, for no good reason other than the sheer delight of the thing, the following "Computation of the most remarkable Passages of the Times, from the Creation, to this present Year 1758":

The Creation of the World, according to Chronology, is 5707

Noah's Flood—4051

Sodom and Gomorrah destroyed by Fire—3659

The Destruction of *Troy*—2942

The Building of the Temple at *Jerusalem*—2775

Brute entered this Island—2865

The Building of *London*—2865

The Building of *Rome*—2809

The Building of *York*—2745

The Building of *Cambridge*, by *Sigisbert*, King of the *East-Angles*—2038

The Bible translated in *Greek* by the Seventy Interpreters, at the Command of
  Ptolemy Philadelphus—2023

Clocks and Dials first set up in Churches—1145

Glasing and Building with Stone brought into *England* by *Bennet*, a Monk—1088

St. *Paul's* Church burnt—582

London-Bridge, after thirty three Years Labour, finished with Stone—549

London-Bridge burnt—544

Tiling first used in *London*—511

A Frost from *September* to *April*—484

The first Use of Guns—378

Printing first used in *England*—305

Register Books in every Parish—259

The Sweating Sickness—227

The first Use of Coaches—205

The last Firing of St. *Paul's* Steeple—197

A great Frost and sudden Thaw, which broke many Bridges—192

The *Royal Exchange* finished—187

A Blazing Star in *May*—178

A great Plague whereof died in one Year, in *London*, 30,578 Persons—154

J

Dear Old Father William,

I read with interest the transcription of the Donizetti autopsy report. My opera club—we have been meeting once a month for almost forty years, by the way—is devoting this whole year to a study of Donizetti, focusing on some of the lesser-known works, of which there are a considerable number. You may know that he was one of the many composers whose troubles were rooted in syphilitic contagion. He made his career in Paris, and he endured a long and enforced confinement there, in a kind of locked-ward situation, before persistent efforts on the part of his nephew enabled him to return to Bergamo, Italy, to die and, subsequently, be anatomized in the tool shed.

Among the panel of three physicians who signed the document attesting that the composer was not mentally competent to travel

J

was the Philadelphia-born Philippe Ricord, who took his practice to Paris and became the leading venereologist of his day. It's for him that Ricord's chancre, a characteristic syphilitic sore, is named; also the Ricord speculum, employed for gynecological examination.

For your information,

J.N.

Namesake Specula

Cusco's Speculum

Dr. Cusco's device came on stream in the mid-nineteenth century, the Golden Age of speculum development, around about the same time as Seyffert, Collin, and Trelat were putting their names on their specula and their specula on the quite crowded market. Cusco was a French physician who was inspired— Heaven knows by what set of circumstances—to draft up and manufacture a two-pronged, "duck-bill" instrument. Luckily, his mother tongue didn't leave him vulnerable to accusations of quackery, although the phrase "the same old canard" might have been brought to bear.

Sims's Speculum

James Marion Sims is known as "the father of American gynecology," though if ever a profession required a mother, this would surely be the one. The Sims position—the on-the-side, knees-tucked-up-to-the-chest posture used in some vaginal and rectal examinations—was also his innovation; new parents debating the merits of one name over another might want to note what can happen when you saddle your son with the middle moniker "Marion." Sims was born on January 25, currently Burns Day, but which might also be named Sims Day in honour of the joy he brought to the world.

Thudicum's Speculum

The rhinologist's best friend is used for nasal examination, and named for Dr. J.W.L. Thudicum, to whose book on gastronomy, *Cookery: Its Art and Practice*, I have often referred.

Bowman's Speculum

The English ophthalmologist Dr. Bowman introduced this instrument round about 1853 as a way of getting around obstructions of the tear ducts.

Barraquer's Speculum

Also of ophthalmological interest, this device was named for Ignacio Barraquer, "the father of modern refractive surgery" and founder of the Catalan School of Ophthalmology. A pioneer in cataract removal, he performed more than thirty thousand operations over his long career. He is said to have invented his suction method of removing cataracts after observing a leech in an aquarium latch onto a small stone; for what purpose, we're not sure—perhaps to hurl it at the glass of the aquarium, thus avoiding the possibility of being press-ganged into barometric service (see *How to Make a Leech Barometer*). Barraquer maintained a small private zoo on the grounds of his clinic.

Avery's Speculum

In 1844, John Avery, a surgeon at Charing Cross Hospital, London, wanted a better way to peer into the throat. His solution was a head-mounted mirror and a candle reflected onto another mirror mounted on his speculum, which combination allowed him an improved view.

Ferguson's Speculum

William Ferguson, an English practitioner of the early nineteenth century, introduced mirrored specula into the always cheerful and reflective world of gynecology.

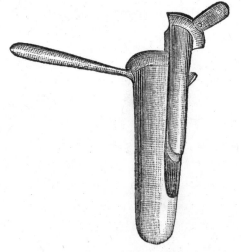

Dr. Hilton's Rectal Speculum: Divide and Conquer!

And here, just to ice the specula-tive cake, are some other eponymous medical instruments:

- Heinrich Fritsch. **Fritsch's skin hook**, used for the hooking of skin.
- William Hey. **Hey's saw**, designed with the skull in mind. Hey crippled himself getting out of the bath.
- Greenfield Sluder. **Sluder's snare**, used for the snaring of tonsils.
- John Benjamin Murphy. **Murphy's button**, used for intestinal anastomosis.
- Alfred Washington Adson. **Beckman-Adson retractor**, used for keeping a wound open while it's dealt with. But who was Beckman?
- Johann Friedrich Horner. **Horner's hollow chisel**, useful for removing from the cornea bits of things that don't belong there.
- Charles Philamore Bailey. **Bailey's forceps**, which have an "intraventricular" application, which may or may not mean that they are used without moving the lips.
- Harvey Williams Cushing. **Cushing's clip**, a small silver clip invented in 1910, presumably for neurosurgical use, but perhaps just to wear out on special occasions.
- Richard von Volkmann. **Volkmann's spoon**, a sharpened spoon used to scrape away from the bone stuff that needs scraping away.

•

This "bright" from the *Cincinnati Lancet* was reproduced in the *Scientific American* (December 19, 1885). It has nothing to do with specula, but describes another method of enforced dilation.

Dr. Grangier, surgeon in the French army, writes from Algeria: "A few days after the occupation of Brizerte, when the military authorities had forbidden, under the severest penalties, the discharge of firearms within the town, the whole garrison was awakened at three o'clock one morning by the tremendous explosion of a heavily loaded gun in the neighbor- hood of the ramparts; a guard of soldiers rushed into the house from whence the sound had come, and found a woman lying on the floor with a newly born babe between her thighs. The father of the child stood over his wife with the smoking musket still in his hand, but his intentions in firing the gun had been wholly medical, and not hostile to the French troops. The husband discovered that his wife had been in labor for thirty-six hours. Labor was slow and the contractions weak and far apart. He had thought it advisable to provoke speedy contraction, and, following the Algerian custom to scare the baby out, he had fired the musket near his wife's ear; instantaneously the accouchement was terminated. After being imprisoned twenty-four hours, the Arab was released."

"You are old," said the youth, "and your jaws are too weak
For anything tougher than suet;
Yet you finished the goose, with the bones and the beak—
Pray, how did you manage to do it?"

"In my youth," said his father, "I took to the law,
And argued each case with my wife;
And the muscular strength, which it gave to my jaw,
Has lasted the rest of my life."

Clothes horse upset by a monkey.

Fires and Their Causes

Mr. Braidwood's report, which was published in the *Eclectic Magazine of Foreign Literature, Science and Art,* includes the following table charting fires in London since the establishment of the fire brigade there. Old Father William is especially intrigued by conflagrations owing to "smoking ants" and "clotheshorse upset by monkey."

Curtains	2,511		Candle	1,178
Flues	1,555		Stoves	494
Gas	932		Light dropped down Area	13
Lighted Tobacco falling down ditto	7		Dust falling on horizontal Flue	1
Doubtful	76		Incendiarism	89
Carelessness	100		Intoxication	80
Dog	6		Cat	19
Hunting Bugs	15		Clotheshorse upset by Monkey	1
Lucifers	80		Children playing with ditto	45
Jackdaw playing with ditto	1		Rat gnawing gaspipe	1
Boys letting off Fireworks	14		Fireworks going off	63
Children playing with Fire	45		Spark from Fire	243
Spark from Railway	4		Smoking Tobacco	166
Smoking Ants	1		Smoking in Bed	2
Reading in ditto	22		Sewing in ditto	4
Sewing by Candle	1		Lime overheating	44
Waste ditto	43		Cargo of Lime ditto	2
Rain Slacking ditto	5		High Tide	1
Explosion	6		Spontaneous Combustion	43
Heat from Sun	8		Lightning	8
Carboy of Acid bursting	2		Drying Linen	1
Shirts falling into fire	6		Lighting and Upsetting Naphtha Lamp	58
Fire from Iron Kettle	1		Sealing Letter	1
Charcoal Fire of a Suicide	1		Insanity	5
Bleaching Nuts	7		Unknown	1,323

Mr. Braidwood also lists the following trades as "too hazardous to be insured at any price":

floor-cloth manufacturers

hatters' "stock in the stove"

lucifer-match makers

wadding-manufacturers

gunpowder dealers

lamp-black makers

varnish-makers

The following are considered highly hazardous:

bone-crushers

composition-ornament makers

dyers

flambeau-makers

hemp and flax dressers

japanners and japan-makers

patent japan-leather manufacturers

rough-fat melters

oil and color men

oiled silk and linen makers

pitch-makers

resin-dealers

seed-crushers

soap-makers

sugar-refiners

thatched houses in towns

coffee-roasters

curriers

feather-stovers

heckling-houses

ivory-black makers

laboratory-chemists

lint-mills

musical-instrument makers

leather-dressers

oil of vitriol manufacturers

rag-dealers

saw-mills

ship-biscuit bakers

spermaceti and wax refiners

tar dealers and boilers

turpentine-makers

Instructions for better living

How Not to Catch Fire

Dancers, and those that are accustomed to wear light muslins and other inflammable articles of clothing, when they are likely to come in contact with the gas, would do well to remember, that by steeping them in a solution of alum they would not be liable to catch fire. If the rule were enforced at theatres, we might avoid any possible recurrence of such a catastrophe as happened at Drury Lane in 1844, when poor Clara Webster was so burnt before the eyes of the audience, that she died in a few days.

—"Fires and Firemen: Annual Reports of Mr. Braidwood
to the Committee of the Fire Brigade" (1855)

I

Dear Old Father William,

Further to the business about poor Clara Webster,
the ballerina who died a terrible death when her
costume caught on fire, you might be interested
to learn that a similar fate befell the French
ballerina Emma Livry, who declined to use the
available flame retardants because they caused
the tulle of her costumes to go yellow and stiff.
She died of injuries incurred when she came
into contact with a gas jet at the Paris ballet in
1863. Livry was especially well known for her
performances in Les Sylphides.

I recall reading somewhere that during a
performance of Les Sylphides, during which
ballet the sylph is intended to fly up the chimney,
the ballerina—I believe it was the great Dutch
prima, Martine van Hamel—became stuck
in the flue. Her lower extremities were left
exposed to the audience and, in the spirit of

J

the show going on, she kept her legs moving in entrechat after entrechat until the curtain came down and she could be pried loose. Perhaps some kind of heavy-duty, jaws-of-life speculum was employed.

I hope you find this useful, although I find myself thinking that "useful" is about the last thing it could ever be.

J.N.

A Bad Case of the Flue

The moral of the story, I suppose, is that life in the theatre is fraught with peril. One imagines that Miss van Hamel, or whoever the ballerina, was fairly easily extracted from the stage prop chimney. St. Nicholas, in the Clement Moore poem about his Christmas Eve visit, passes easily up and down the sooty passageway. It isn't so handy a means of access or egress for everyone who gives it a try.

•

On Christmas morning 2003, police were called to Uncle Hugo's Bookstore, in Minneapolis, to dislodge **Joseph Hubbert** from the chimney. When asked by the investigating officers to explain himself, Mr Hubbert stated that he had dropped his keys. He was in a state of semi-undress at the time of his sooty re-emergence.

•

In June 1993, **William Quinga**, who also goes by the name **William Vermeo**, tried to enter Luigi Italian Restaurant, in the Jackson Heights neighbourhood of New York, via the chimney. He became stuck. Police and firefighters arrived at the scene and quarrelled, rather violently, about how Mr. Vermeo/Quinga should be removed, and who should do it. The firefighters wanted to haul him out the top; the police wanted to smash through the bricks. In the end, the police prevailed.

•

Michael Urbano was "naked as a jaybird," according to police lieutenant Gary Branson, when the rescue squad extracted him from his stepmother's chimney in Hayward, California, on April 23, 2006. Mr. Urbano had locked himself out of the house and removed his duds in order to "reduce friction." He was taken to the hospital, treated for abrasions, and arrested on the suspicion that intoxicants may have been involved.

•

In July 1994, **David Moore** was arrested in New Haven, Connecticut, after he became stuck in a chimney while trying to rob a convenience store. In a possible demonstration of biology as destiny, it was the self-same convenience store where his brother, Richard, had become entrapped in the ceiling several years before, also while feloniously employed.

•

It took firefighters four hours to cut through the chimney in which **Marco Espinoza** became stuck after trying to illegally enter the house of Danny and Nelia Ramos, of West Covina, California.

•

The following inspiring tale was told by William Andrus Alcott in *The Young Woman's Guide* (1840). Dr. Alcott, a cousin to Bronson Alcott and his daughter Louisa May, was the first president of the American Vegetarian Society; it's difficult to imagine, somehow, that Mrs. Merrill was anything other than an enthusiastic meat eater:

> Some thirty or forty years ago, when the Indians had not yet done making depredations on the inhabitants of our then frontier states, Kentucky and Ohio, a band of these savage men came to the door of a house in Nelson county, Ky., and having shot down the father of the little family within, who had incautiously opened the door, they attempted to rush in and put to death the defence-less and unoffending mother and her children. But Mrs. Merrill—for that was the name of the

heroic woman—had much of that self-command, or presence of mind, which was now so needful. She drew her wounded husband into the house, closed the door and barred it as quickly as possible, so that the Indians could not enter at once, and then proceeded to the defence of "her castle," and all those in it whom she held dear.

The **Indians** had soon hewed away a part of the door, so that they could force themselves in, one by one, but not very rapidly. This slow mode of entrance gave time to Mrs. M. to despatch them with an axe, and drag them in; so that before those without were aware of the fate of those inside, she had, with a little assistance from her husband, formed quite a pile of dead bodies within and around the door; and even the little children, half dead though they at first were with fear, had gradually begun to recover from their fright.

The Indians, finding their party so rapidly disappearing, at length began to suspect what was their fate, and accordingly gave up their efforts in that direction. They now attempted to descend into the house by way of the chimney. The united wisdom and presence of mind of the family was again put in requisition, and they emptied upon the fire the contents of a feather bed, which brought down, half smothered, those Indians that were in the chimney, who were also soon and easily despatched. The remainder of the party, now very much reduced in numbers, became quite discouraged, and concluded it was best to retire.

Progress of Refinement in America

INDIANS' SCALPS

Pittsburg, May 17, 1791

We the subscribers, encouraged by a large subscription, do promise to pay One Hundred Dollars for every hostile Indian's scalp, with both ears to it, taken between this date and the 15th day of June next, by any inhabitant of Alleghany county.

George Wallace
Robert Elliot
Wm. Amberson
A. Tannehill
J. Wilkins, jun.
John Irwin

Henry Mason Brooks, *The Olden Times Series, Quaint and Curious Advertisements, Gleanings Chiefly from Old Newspapers of Boston and Salem, Massachusetts* (1886)

When Wigs Go Wrong

Wigs can be more trouble than they're worth, certainly. In the *British Journal* (1763), we find the following evidence. Pedants please note that the aberrant spellings are original to the text.

It is reported that the late invented white gun-powder has hitherto done more mischief than good. A necessitous barber obtaining a quantity and imagining it to be a powder for the hair, took an opportunity of removing it, and at an Assembly at Lyons, in France, a Gentleman at a card table whose wig had been unfortunately powdered with it, standing too near the candles, the powder unfortunately took fire, blasted the faces of the Company terribly and by the sudden contraction and distortion of their features gave them a most ridiculous appearance, which they were likely to carry to their graves. The Gentleman's head was burnt in such a manner that only a small portion of the cartaliginous substance of the ears remained and the skin of the head peeled off entirely and the surtures of the scull were all plainly to be discovered as in a skelaton. It is said he is since dead.

Old Father William calls that "speaking truth to powder." Here are some other examples of wigging out.

•

Andy Warhol.

+

Cher

+

Bobby Hull.

Wigs gone wrong.

In 2003, during a farewell tour that may well hold the record for world's longest goodbye, **Cher**, the pop diva, had a braided black-and-teal wig stolen from her dressing room at the Richmond Coliseum, in Virginia. It was reserved for her use during performances of "All or Nothing," and was valued at ten thousand dollars; it was surely worth more when its provenance was taken into account. After a few days on the lam, the hairpiece was returned.

•

On October 30, 1985, while he was signing copies of *America* at the Rizzoli Bookstore in New York City, **Andy Warhol** suffered the indignation of having his wig torn from his head by a souvenir hunter. She tossed the piece to her friend and they made off with it. Happily, Warhol's coat, by Calvin Klein, had a hood and he was able to go on signing. At a Christie's auction in 2006, Warhol's wig—presumably not the one made off with by the felons, who were very lucky they weren't living in eighteenth-century England—sold for $10,800. Cher fans, upset at the $800 discrepancy in value, should note that Warhol's rug included three pieces of toupée tape.

•

A Harris hawk named Harry, star of a wildlife show given at the Thorp Perrow Arboretum, near Bedale, in North Yorkshire, was stricken from the roster after fifteen years of service after he snatched a toupée from the head of a spectator. In March 2003, the BBC reported that the theft occurred during a "dummy bunny" routine when a piece of brown fur was thrown into the audience for him to retrieve. Owner Tom Graham said of the shocked victim, "Harry decided to use him as a perch but unfortunately when he took off he still had the toupée in his feet. He tried to eat it and was having a bit of a tear at it." In the past Harry had deflated a bouncy castle and ruined an ice cream vendor's stock by flying into the van. Also in 2003, Izzy, a snowy owl, made off with the wig of a visitor to the Gentleshaw Wildlife Centre in Staffordshire. The wig was retrieved.

•

The most glorious wig debacle ever imagined, the *ne plus ultra* of unravelled perruquery, can be found in the pages of Jacqueline Susann's *Valley of the Dolls*. I refer to the episode in the lady's room of the swanky nightclub, where **Neely O'Hara**, recently released from rehab and on the showbiz comeback trail, engages Broadway veteran **Helen Lawson** in a cat fight. Helen's wig is ripped off in the melee, and Neely attempts to flush it down the loo. Neely comes out on top, but Helen more than redeems herself with the line, "They drummed you out of Hollywood, so you come crawling back to Broadway. But Broadway doesn't go for booze and dope. Now get out of my way, I've got a man waiting for me!" The film version, starring Patty Duke and Susan Hayward, offers a memorable depiction of this, one of the most thrilling moments in all of American literature.

•

In 1978, during a World Hockey Association game between the Winnipeg Jets and the Birmingham Bulls, **Bobby Hull's** toupée was wrested from his scalp in an on-ice dust-up with either Steve Durbano or Dave Hanson. That the truth of the matter is so elusive—was it Durbano or Hanson, was it the game of March 12 or April 14, was the rug thrown into the stands or cast down on the ice or sliced to ribbons by vengeful blades?—is an excellent demonstration of how quickly myths are made and how we value a story more than we value the truth.

{ **Andy Warhol suffered the indignation of having his wig torn from his head by a souvenir hunter.** }

•

While shooting "San Francisco," episode 28 of the first season of *Bonanza*, in 1960, **Lorne Greene**, playing a shanghaied Ben Cartwright, was dunked in a vast water tank. Greene was submerged but his hairpiece remained on the surface. Michael Landon, telling the story to Johnny Carson on the *Tonight Show*, said that Greene simply refused to come up for air until he'd managed to grab the rug and replace it.

•

In 1997, sportscaster **Marv Albert** went to trial for forcing his attentions on his long-time associate Vanessa Perhach. The alleged episode, which involved fifteen bite marks to the back—of Miss Perhach—took place in a Ritz-Carlton hotel in Pentagon City, Virginia. One of the witnesses called by the prosecution was Patricia Masten, an employee of the Hyatt hotel chain. She recalled how, once upon a time when Mr. Albert had been a guest at her establishment, he had summoned her to his room to assist him with "faxing a letter." He was wearing panties and a garter belt when she arrived, which is not unusual attire in which to find a guest, but when he began to chomp at her neck she thought it best to retire. Miss Masten held the court in thrall with her account of how she attempted to fend off his advances by grabbing Mr. Albert's toupée. It came away, which created a diversion of sufficient magnitude that she was able to beat a retreat. Mr. Albert was de-furred, and his sentence was suspended.

•

On May 31, 2004, the *New York Post* reported, "Coney Island Cyclone riders had a hair-raising experience yesterday when the world-famous roller coaster stopped dead in its tracks at the top of a hill after a woman's wig blew off and got caught in the wheels. The bizarre mishap had riders stuck in their seats for nearly 30 minutes." The wig was never claimed by its owner.

•

While shooting *Bonanza*, Lorne Greene was submerged in a water tank, but his hairpiece remained on the surface.

Thomas Busby, in *Concert Room and Orchestra Anecdotes* (1825), has this account of Baroque composer **George Handel**'s wig gone awry:

Handel's nerves were too irritable to stand the sound of tuning, and his players therefore tuned their instruments before he arrived. One evening, when the Prince of Wales was expected to be present, some wag, for a piece of fun, untuned them all. When the Prince arrived, Handel gave the signal to begin con spirito, but such was the horrible discord that the enraged conductor started up from his seat, and, having over-turned a double-bass that stood in the way, seized a kettle-drum and threw it with such force at the leader of the violins that he lost his wig in the effort. Without waiting to replace it, he strode bareheaded to the front of the orchestra, breathing vengeance, but so choked with passion that he could hardly utter a word. In this ridiculous attitude he stood staring and stamping for some moments, amidst the general convulsion of laughter. Nor could he be prevailed upon to resume his seat until the Prince went in person and succeeded in appeasing his wrath.

●

Reverend Brewer, in his *Reader's Handbook*, says that **Catherine the Great** kept her wigmaker in a cage so that he wouldn't be free to reveal to the peasantry, or whoever else might care to know, that the Empress wore a wig.

●

Ned Rorem, the American composer, who kept a diary during his years in Paris, describes a visit to the Polish virtuoso **Wanda Landowska**. He'd gone to show her his harpsichord concertino, but the moment he entered the room she unpinned her hair, which fell "in waves to her waist. 'Take it,' she said, 'take it in handfuls and pull it, pull it hard! And never go tell people I wear a wig.'"

●

In *Notes and Queries* (1864) is mention of a discovery that came to light when the church of St. Bartholomew the Great was demolished: "A whole deposit

Wigs of the Eighteenth Century

While we have hair in mind, consider that in England, in the mid-eighteenth century, these thirty-four styles of perruque were in circulation.

Artichoke
Bag
Barrister's
Bishop's
Brush
Buckle chain
Busby
Bush
Chancellor's
Corded wolf's paw
Count Saxes's mode
Crutch
Cut bob
Detached buckle
Drop
Dutch
Full
Half natural
Jansenist bob
Judge's
Ladder
Long bob
Louis
Periwig
Pigeon's wing
Rhinoceros
Rose
Royal bird
Scratch
She-dragon
Small back
Spinage seed
Staircase
Welsh
Wild Boar's Back

of small earthenware sticks was found in one place—all of them exactly alike, about five inches long and in shape something like a thin baluster. The authorities of the British Museum pronounced at once that they were wig-curlers! It would seem as though some defunct hairdresser of Queen Anne's time had chosen to be buried in his wig, with the curling-pin in each curl."

•

The following account of a labour-related wig donnybrook appears in William Andrews's 1904 book, *At the Sign of the Barber Pole: Studies in Hirsute History:*

On February 11th, 1765, a curious spectacle was witnessed in the streets of London, and one which caused some amusement. Fashion had changed; the peruke was no longer in favour, and only worn to a limited extent. A large number of **peruke-makers** had been thrown out of employment, and distress prevailed amongst them. The sufferers thought that help might be obtained from George III., and a petition was accordingly drawn up for the enforcement of gentlefolk to wear wigs for the benefit of the wig-makers. A procession was formed, and waited upon the king at St James's Palace. His Majesty, it is said, returned a gracious answer, but it must have cost him considerable effort to maintain his gravity.

Besides the monarch, the unemployed had to encounter the men of the metropolis, and we learn from a report of the period they did not fare so well. "As the distressed men went processionally through the town," says the account, "it was observed that most of the wig-makers, who wanted other people to wear them, wore no wigs themselves; and this striking the London mob as something monstrously unfair and inconsistent, they seized the petitioners, and cut off all their hair per force."

Horace Walpole alludes to this ludicrous petition in one of his letters. "Should we wonder," he writes, "if carpenters were to remonstrate that since the Peace there is no demand for wooden legs?" The wags of the period could not allow the opportunity to pass without attempting to provoke more mirth out of the matter, and a petition was published purporting to come from the body-carpenters imploring his Majesty to wear a wooden leg, and to enjoin his servants to appear in his royal presence with the same graceful decoration.

Legendary Legs
and Where They Were Pegged

Treasure Island is set in the mid-eighteenth century, just around the time the wig-makers launched their short-lived campaign and drew the scorn of Horace Walpole. Wigs and wooden legs both figure in Stevenson's creation: the treasure-hungry Dr. Livesey wears the former and the piratical Long John Silver the latter. Long John is one of the most celebrated prosthetic wearers, factual or fictive, but he's in excellent company.

•

Thomas Askins was an eighteenth-century English ex-serviceman who, having lost a leg in the service of King and country round about the time Long John mislaid his own limb, apparently used his wooden leg as a kind of primitive seed drill, tamping out holes for the planting of potatoes. He went on to become a pioneer in the art of ventriloquism.

•

Clayton "Peg-Leg" Bates (1907–89) had no qualms about using his wooden leg in surprising ways. Bates, who tap-danced his way into the heart of America on the *Ed Sullivan Show* (twenty-two appearances) was eleven years old when he lost his left leg in the conveyor belt of a cotton separator. Determined not to let the severing become a disability, he set out to prove himself able bodied in every way. As his career as a dancer evolved, he acquired thirty-six different legs, coloured to match his suits. One of his signature routines was the "Jet Plane," which required him to dash across the stage, leap into the air, land on the prosthetic, and bounce in time to the orchestra. He was an expert leaper and claimed that on days when he was in excellent trim, he could jump his whole height—five foot eleven—and make a complete turn. Mindful of the colour bar that banned African American tourists from the various clubs of the Catskills, Clayton and his wife, Alice, opened the Peg-Leg Bates Country Club in upstate New York.

•

Peter Stuyvesant (1612–72), governor of New Amsterdam (on the southern tip of the island of Manhattan), lost his leg in a battle with the Spanish in 1644. His wooden leg was driven through with silver nails, one supposes for aesthetic reasons: hence his sobriquet "Old Silver Nails." (James Cagney is among the alumni of Stuyvesant School, in New York City, which was founded in 1904.)

•

The same year, 1904, was when **George Eyser**, aged thirty-three, took his wooden leg to the St. Louis Olympics and captured six medals in gymnastics. He took gold in rope climbing, vault, and parallel bars, silver in pommel horse and the combined four events, and bronze in horizontal bar. Eyser lost his left leg in a train accident.

•

On September 21, 2007, Long Beach, California, resident **Jereme James** was indicted for smuggling three hatchling Fiji banded iguanas (*Brachylophus fasciatus*) into the United States, concealed in a compartment he had constructed in his prosthetic leg. He had abducted them from a Fijian ecological preserve and sold them stateside, in a sting operation, for thirty-two thousand dollars.

•

London Life Magazine, between 1924 and 1941, published over three hundred stories, articles, and letters about the relative special attraction of one-legged young women. The stories—with such titles as "Famous though Limbless"—were the work of "Wallace Stort" and the letters came from any number of sympathetic correspondents. For example:

Dear Sir,—the following may interest your one-legged readers and those who are admirers of their pluck and their attractive appearance.

Recently I was roaming through London and noticed a girl, good-looking, smartly dressed and minus her right leg, hopping along on two crutches. Her one leg was well dressed in a silk stocking and she wore a high heeled Court shoe. While standing on the up-going **escalator** at Leicester Square station, I was amazed to see this girl gracefully mounting it whilst it was in motion, at a much greater speed than many able bodied people. She seemed to swing herself along with complete confidence, and appeared to be oblivious of her crippled state.

There was something extremely attractive about this girl having only one well dressed leg, and her only foot so neatly shod in her brown high-heeled Court shoe.

Why girls who have lost a leg should wish to wear an artificial one, I cannot understand; for they are far more attractive on their crutches. But this is only a mere man's point of view.

During the same "roam" I saw another girl using crutches, but this one was not minus a leg; but her left leg was perhaps 24 inches short—too short fortunately, for her to wear any unsightly boot or irons.

When the first escalators at a tube station were installed at Earl's Court in 1911, the public was alarmed and disinclined to use them. **Bumper Harris**, who had a wooden leg, was engaged to ride up and down on the escalator all day long, to prove that they were quite safe, even for the unlimbed. His wages were fifteen pence per day.

This leg hung limply, gently swaying as she moved along. Her left foot hung downwards (due to a stiff instep), and disclosed a Court shoe of patent leather with a heel which must have been 5 inches high. The shoe, of course, looked perfect, as it was not even soiled owing to her inability to use it or to touch the ground with it. This, too, was another form of attractiveness in a hopelessly lame girl.

I have observed other girls compelled to use crutches, either due to shortness of a leg or to the amputation of one, but I will not describe those unless your readers wish it, as it is already a long letter.

It is, however, sufficient to show that most crippled or one-legged girls, especially when well dressed, incite the admiration and sympathy of

Yours truly,
A Mere Male

•

Josiah Wedgwood (1730–95), the founder of the pottery that bears his name, had his right leg amputated above the knee on May 26, 1768. The leg may have been damaged by the lingering effects of the smallpox he had contracted as a boy. A Mr. Addison, whose business was making lay figures—jointed wooden mannequins—for artists, made Wedgwood's first prosthetic limb. Wedgwood was the grandfather of Charles Darwin.

•

Charles Dickens, Darwin's almost exact contemporary—there were three years between them—was fascinated to the point of obsession by wooden legs. In volume 171 of *Notes and Queries* (August 22, 1936), G. Crosse contributes an exhaustive catalogue of peg-legs in Dickens's oeuvre: dozens and dozens, seemingly. We'll settle on this one example, from the "Report of the Committee of the Brick Lane Branch of the United Grand Junction Ebenezer Temperance Association" in *The Pickwick Papers*:

> Thomas Burton is purveyor of cat's meat to the Lord Mayor and Sheriffs, and several members of the Common Council (the announcement of this gentleman's name was received with breathless interest). Has a wooden leg; finds a wooden leg expensive, going over the stones; used to wear second-hand wooden legs, and drink a glass of hot gin-and-water regularly every night—sometimes two (deep sighs). Found the second-hand wooden legs split and rot very quickly; is firmly persuaded that their constitution was undermined by the gin-and-water (prolonged cheering). Buys new wooden legs now, and drinks nothing but water and weak tea. The new legs last twice as long as the others used to do, and he attributes this solely to his temperate habits (triumphant cheers).

•

Sarah Bernhardt, the legendary French actress, had her leg amputated in 1915. She was fitted with a wooden leg, but rarely relied on it; for the six years left to her, she preferred to be borne about in a sedan chair. On November 6 in the year of her *déjambement*, a reporter for the *New York Times* filed a special cable on Bernhardt's return to the stage "and her debut with her wooden leg" in the verse play *Les Cathédrales*, by Eugène Morand. She portrayed Strasbourg Cathedral, an assignment that would have been daunting for the sturdiest biped.

It has often been reported that P.T. Barnum offered to purchase the severed leg for ten thousand dollars, with a view to putting it on display in some pre-serving liquid. However, as Barnum died in 1891, this seems unlikely, unless mediumship was in some way implicated.

•

Finally, I give you this story from the *New York Times* (July 27, 1922):

Chiropractor Dies in Ten-Story Leap

Immediately after conversing cheerfully with several acquaintances yesterday afternoon in the building at the northeast corner of Madison Avenue and Thirty-fourth Street, Archer R. Johns, a chiropractor, who had a large suite of offices on the fourth floor, climbed six more flights of stairs and leaped from a tenth-story window. Some of the passersby in the shopping and luncheon throngs had narrow escapes from injury when the body dropped among them on the sidewalk. Johns had a wooden leg which made a terrific noise on the pavement.

I

Dear Old Father William,

Here's a book that's no longer required by the youth section of the public library, Secrets of Magic, by Walter Gibson. It was Mr. Gibson who originated the character of The Shadow, of old-time radio fame; not even I am old enough to have known The Shadow first hand, but his reputation endures.

One of the pleasures of my job is that it allows me into all the subterranean hidey-holes that are forbidden to civilian library users. I spend days at a stretch in remote, and sometimes rather dank, storage areas where no other living, breathing person has trod, or so it seems, for a very long time. I quite literally squint in the light when I emerge from my cave at day's end. It's a solitary undertaking that wouldn't do for most, but it suits me nicely. There are times, it's true, when I dally longer over a book or periodical

I

than is strictly necessary to make my keep-it-
or-turf-it determination. Last week I spent a
very happy couple of hours leafing through the
bound volumes of the Journal of the American
Temperance Union. I was reminded of your
account of persons who became stuck in chimneys,
many—if not all—of whom were inebriated at
the time of their unfortunate wedging. They would
do well to note, given their proximity to possible
heat, that most cases of spontaneous human
combustion are visited on persons who drink to
excess; and they might also want to read closely
this story, from the Temperance Union journal,
about a sad episode that took place in Upper
Canada, as it was called in 1837. The writer is one
Dr. Schofield.

Those were the days of vivid writing, Old Father
William. Those were surely the days.

J.N.

Instructions for better living

DISCOVER THE LIGHT WITHIN

A most convincing and spectacular torture trick performed by Indian fakirs is the lighting of a fire on a boy's head. The fakir exhibits a large clay cylinder with both ends open; this he places on the boy's head to serve as a fire box, and into it he stuffs paper, rags, bits of wood, and even pours oil on top. Then the fakir sets fire to the contents of the cylinder, still adding fuel as the flames spurt upward with increasing fury from the boy's head. Yet the boy remains unperturbed, apparently immune to the scorching heat. This is attributed to the fakir's magical powers. And when the fire has subsided, the fakir dumps the ashes from the cylinder and shows it empty as before. The boy's head is quite unharmed, and the fakir pats it and sends him happily on his way.

Not only is it a trick, it is a very simple one, which is true of many good tricks. In packing fuel into the cylinder, the fakir introduces a flat disc of thick clay. The interior of the cylinder tapers slightly inward and the fakir takes care that the smaller end is placed upon the boy's head. As a result, the disk becomes wedged as it slides downward, as it is just a trifle larger than the smaller end of the cylinder.

This confines the fire to the upper portion of the cylinder, with an air space between the clay portion and the boy's head. With the disc properly wedged, the boy scarcely notices the heat as the fire constantly burns upward. At the finish, the fakir removes the cylinder, turns it over and dumps out the clay disk with the ashes and no one is wiser. Occasionally, a fakir cooks a meal above the blazing chimney while it is still on the boy's head, making the effect all the more remarkable.

—Walter Gibson, *Secrets of Magic* (1973)

Spontaneous Combustion

A young man, aged twenty-five, had been an habitual drunkard for many years. One evening at about eleven o'clock he went to a blacksmith's shop: he was then full of liquor, though not thoroughly drunk. The blacksmith, who had just crossed the road, was suddenly alarmed by the breaking forth of a brilliant conflagration in his shop. He rushed across, and threw open the door, and there stood the man, erect, in the midst of a widely-extended silver-coloured flame, bearing, as he described it, exactly the appearance of the wick of a burning candle in the midst of its own flame. He seized him by the shoulder, and jerked him to the door, and the flame was instantly extinguished. There was no fire in the shop, and no articles likely to cause combustion within reach of the individual. In the course of a short time a general sloughing came on, and the flesh was almost wholly removed in the dressing, leaving the bones and a few of the large blood-vessels standing. The blood nevertheless rallied round the heart, and life continued to the thirteenth day, when he died, a loathsome, ill-featured, and disgusting object. His shrieks and cries were described as truly horrible.

Speaking of spontaneous combustion, the table on page 140 can be found in *Notes and Queries* (May 7, 1853). Compiled by James Shirley Hibberd, whose main line of inquiry was botany, it seems to corroborate the theory that spontaneous human combustion and alcohol are linked, and suggests to Old Father William that, contrary to the proverb, sometimes it is better simply to curse the darkness.

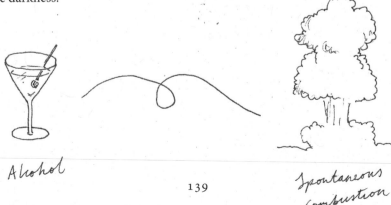

Alcohol

Spontaneous Combustion

Spontaneous Combustion: A Collection of Case Particulars

No.	Works in which they are reported.	By whom.	Date of Occurrence.	Age of the Individual.
1	Actes de Copenhagen	Jacobeus	1692	—
2	Annual Register	Blanchin de Verone	1763	62
3	Ibid.	Wilmer	—	50
4	Ency. Method.	—	—	50
5	Acta Medica	—	—	—
6	Mem. On Spon. Com.	Lecat	1744	60
7	Ibid.	Ibid.	1745	—
8	Ibid.	Ibid.	1749	80
9	Jour. de Méd.	—	1779	—
10	Ibid.	—	1782	60
11	Revue Médicale	Julia Fontenelle	1820	90
12	Ibid.	Ibid.	1830	66
13	—	Gen. William Kepland	—	Very old
14	Journal de Florence	Joseph Battaylia	1786	—
15	Revue Méd.	Robertson	1799	—
16	Ibid.	M. Marchand	—	—
17	Journal Hosp. Hamp.	—	—	17
18	—	Alph. Devengee	1829	51
19	Dic. De Médecine	—	—	—

Extent of the Combustion.	Immediate Cause when known.	Habit of Life.	Situation of the Remains etc.
The whole body, except the skull and last joints of the fingers	—	Abuse of spirits for three years	Upon a chair
Except the skull, a part of the face, and three fingers	Took fire through sitting near a lamp	Indulged in frequent fomentation of camphorated spirits	Upon the floor
Except thigh and one leg	A light upon a chair near the bed	Took a pint of rum daily	Upon the floor near the bed
Except a few bones	—	Habitually drunken.	
Except the skull and fingers	—	She drank brandy as her only drink	
Except a part of the head and limbs	A pipe which she was smoking	A drunkard	Near the chimney
Ibid.	A fire	Habitually drunken	Upon the hearth
A charred skeleton only left	Fire of the hearth	Drank brandy only for many years	Sitting on a chair near the fire
Except a few bones, a hand, and a foot	A foot-stove under her feet	A drunkard.	
Ibid.	A fire of the hearth	Ibid.	Upon the hearth
Except the skull and a portion of skin	A candle	Abuse of wine and Eau de Cologne	In bed
Except the right leg	Ibid.	Ibid.	In the same bed. Both burnt together.
Almost wholly consumed	A lighted pipe	—	Upon the floor
Skin of right arm and right thigh only burnt	—	—	Upon the floor. He lived four days after.
Combustion incomplete	—	Abuse of brandy	Upon a bench
Hand and thigh only burnt	—	—	Cured
One finger of right hand only burnt	A candle	—	Cured
Muscles of thighs, superior extremities and trunk burnt	A footstove	Abuse of spirits	Upon a chair
Combustion almost complete	A footstove	Ibid.	Upon the floor

J

Dear Old Father William,

I've been giving my grandson a hand with
his high school history essay on Stalin, which
makes for cheerful reading. I came across
a footnote—I love a good footnote—that
reminded me of your mention of the composer
Shostakovich, that the themes for several
of his symphonies came to him in dreams.
Apparently, in 1943, Shostakovich was
among the composers who took part in a
Stalin-sponsored competition for the creation
of a new Soviet anthem. Twenty poets and
composers were summoned to attend a June
18 meeting where highly placed bureaucrats
instructed them on what the anthem should
contain and convey. For several hours they
listened to such adumbratory admonishments
as "Its lyrics must live decades at least,
and maybe, and even for sure, hundreds of

J

years. Its music must be easy to understand, expressive, plain for Russians as well as for Kalmyks. People will sing both in joy and in misfortune." The strain they felt in preventing their eyes from rolling back in their heads must have been terrible, don't you think?

That I've been so caught up in things Russian explains the borscht in today's delivery. And that little dollop of white, under separate cover, is sour cream.

J.N.

Haste and Waste:
Another Point of View

Borscht, when delivered via a clothesline in a resealable plastic bag, has about it the look of an emergency surgery supply. Nonetheless, it was delicious, quite the tastiest that's ever come my way: Jane Nurse is a beet poet. I did a bit more research on Shostakovich and the anthem question—I like the idea that I, in turn, might be a footnote in her grandson's essay—and the dream thread she mentioned is woven throughout.

It turns out that the dark-horse winners of the competition were Captain S. Mikhalkov and Major Gabriel Ureklyan, or El-Reghistan in its Armenian form. They were war reporters, and not even among the officially nominated contenders for the prize. Nonetheless, they got wind of it, and one night, El-Reghistan dreamed the inspiring panegyric: "The noble union of free peoples / Great Russia has welded for ever!" Directly upon waking, he hurried over to his friend's house and they got to work. Somehow they got their text to Stalin, who liked it and directed that it be tweaked to fit an extant melody by Alexandrov. This remains the tune that Russians sing today in moments of patriotic fervour, though the dream-time lyrics no longer hold sway.

Shostakovich jotted down his own entry to the competition on July 7, 1943. Whatever sting he might have felt at being passed over may have been mitigated by knowing that on that very same day he produced the piano sketches for one of his largest works, the Symphony no. 8 in C Minor. The symphony itself was written in less than two months, and the third movement he cranked out in just a week. Amazing, especially when you consider there was just a bit of war underway at the time. Many artifacts, cultural and otherwise, of great and enduring worth were similarly hastily produced.

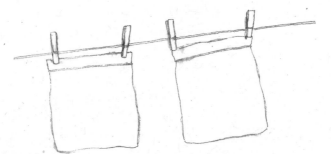

Instructions for better living

HOW TO FIGHT
A DUEL IN RUSSIA

Russian duellists stand fifteen yards apart, and they are allowed to advance five paces at a given signal and fire at will. If both parties advance to the limit before firing, the distance between them is reduced to five yards. Should one fire and miss, the other is allowed to advance his five paces before returning fire. Sometimes one is mortally wounded before firing, but has still sufficient strength left to advance five yards, take steady aim, and shoot his opponent dead.

—*Chambers's Journal* (1897)*

*This was true of the poet Pushkin who, in 1837, was fatally shot in a duel with Baron Georges D'Anthès; mortally wounded, Pushkin had the wherewithal to nick D'Anthès with a returning shot. D'Anthès, who is said to have been wearing a kind of bulletproof vest, recovered nicely and lived another fifty-eight years, dying in 1895. Old Father William cites this as a cautionary example of what can happen when Pushkin comes to Shovekin.

Round about the same time that Shostakovich was composing one of the greatest symphonic statements of the twentieth century, George Orwell was making quick work of his anti-Stalinist satire, **Animal Farm**. It occupied his attention for a mere four months, from November 1943 through February of the following year.

•

It took Sylvester Stallone just three days to write the screenplay that became **Rocky**. The movie went on to win three Oscars, and Stallone became the third person to be nominated for acting and writing in the same year; Charlie Chaplin (*The Great Dictator*) and Orson Welles (*Citizen Kane*) were his predecessors.

•

James Hilton reported that he wrote **Goodbye, Mr. Chips** during a week of fog in London, in November 1933. He said it "was written more quickly, more easily, and with fewer subsequent alterations than anything I have ever written before, or have ever written since."

•

Kurt Vonnegut wrote **Slaughterhouse Five** in six weeks.

•

Tammy Wynette and her writing partner, Bill Sherrill, produced **"Stand by Your Man"** in just fourteen minutes. Which explains rather a lot, actually.

•

In the film *Goldeneye,* Minnie Driver, in a cameo role, sings an off-key version of "Stand by Your Man." Goldeneye was the name of Ian Fleming's Jamaican house (see *Some Thoughts on the Well-Christened Domicile*). That was where he wrote **Casino Royale**, the first of the James Bond novels. It took him eight

Afraid of your bathroom? You should be.
See page 196.

weeks, and spawned a highly successful franchise; more than 100 million copies of the Bond books have been sold, and Lord knows how many action figures.

•

John Osborne wrote **Look Back in Anger** in seventeen days, during which time he was appearing in a play called *Seagulls over Sorrento,* and his wife, Pamela Lane, was getting it on with the local dentist. When Osborne needed two teeth removed, Lane scraped together the cash to pay her lover to do the deed. Presumably, she had every good reason to feel confident about his drilling skills.

•

Bob Wills, of the Texas Playboys, said that he wrote and recorded **"San Antonio Rose"** "in a few minutes" in 1938.

•

The music and lyrics for Pink Floyd's **Dark Side of the Moon** were written in seven weeks. It was on the charts for 591 consecutive weeks, longer than any other album. More than thirty-five million copies have been sold.

•

It took Mel Tormé forty minutes to write the music for **"The Christmas Song"** (made famous by Nat King Cole), on a hot, hot July day in Los Angeles, in 1944. There are more than seventeen thousand recorded versions of that fire-roasted chestnut.

•

Robert Frost, according to Louis Mertins in his book *Robert Frost: Life and Talks-Walking*, wrote **"Stopping by Woods on a Snowy Evening"** in "a few minutes without any strain." He'd spent the evening working on another piece of writing, stepped outside for a break, came back in, and spilled out the famous poem like "a little hallucination."

•

In the preface Larry McMurtry wrote for the 1984 paperback publication of *The Desert Rose*, he said that it was written in a three-week period, at a time when he was lost in the intricacies of writing *Lonesome Dove*.

•

"I met upon glory at 18 years of age in 188 pages. It was like an explosion," said Françoise Sagan, who wrote **Bonjour Tristesse** in six weeks, in 1953. She had just flunked out of the Sorbonne.

•

Another F.S., Franz Schubert, was eighteen when he wrote his **Mass in G Major**. It took him eight days. In that same year, 1815, he wrote over a hundred songs. Robert Winter, in the *New Grove Dictionary of Music*, estimates that Schubert was churning out music at the astonishing rate of sixty-five measures per day.

•

Gioachino Rossini (see *Polly Math*) wrote **The Barber of Seville** in just thirteen days in 1816, which may have given him an odd turn. He was a victim of triskaidekaphobia, the fear of the number thirteen; indeed, he died on November 13, 1868, a Friday. (Oddly enough, Rossini was a leap-year baby, born February 29, 1792.)

•

{ **Gioachino Rossini was a victim of triskaidekaphobia, the fear of the number thirteen.** }

Arnold Schoenberg was prone to paraskavedekatriaphobia, which is the fear of Friday the thirteenth specifically. Schoenberg was born on Friday, September 13, 1874, and died on Friday, July 13, 1951. His astrologer had warned him to anticipate this outcome, as he was in his seventy-sixth year; thirteen is, of course, the sum of seven and six. Schoenberg completed the score of his opera *Erwartung* in seventeen days, in 1909.

•

Vladimir Nabokov wrote ***Invitation to a Beheading*** in Berlin, in 1934, in what the author described as a "fortnight of wonderful excitement and sustained inspiration."

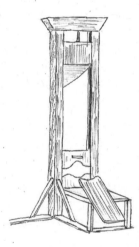

A Highly Selective Survey of Pre-Decapitory Utterances

Jayne Mansfield's last words, before she pitched through the windshield of the Buick Electra 225 in which she took her final ride, went unmarked. By and large, however, beheading comes with sufficient foreknowledge to allow for the calculation and delivery of summary remarks. Here are a few, gathered from diverse sources. Some are more specious than others: *caveat lector.*

•

Charles I, whose head was lopped from his shoulders on January 31, 1649, said, "I go from a corruptible to an incorruptible crown, where no disturbance can be, no disturbance in the world."

•

Josefa Llanes Escoda, founder of the Girl Scout movement in the Philippines, was beheaded by the Japanese in 1945. She said, "Tell our people that the women of the Philippines did their part in keeping the ember sparks of truth and liberty alive till the last moment."

•

In July of 1553, **Lady Jane Grey** logged nine days as Queen of England. She was beheaded on February 12, 1554. She said, "Lord, into thy hands I commend my spirit!"

•

Marie Antoinette showed a studied courtliness when she apologized to the executioner after treading on his toe. "Monsieur, I beg your pardon," was, reportedly her sign-off. Legend has it that her hair turned white the night before the execution.

•

{ **The lips of Mary, Queen of Scots, stirred up and down a quarter of an hour after she was beheaded.** }

Mary, Queen of Scots' grey hair was remarked with surprise by those who witnessed her beheading on February 8, 1587. Note the mention of the removal of her "dress of lawn," i.e., wig, in Robert Wynkfield's contemporary account:

> One of the women having a Corpus Christi cloth lapped up three-corner-ways, kissing it, put it over the Queen of Scots' face, and pinned it fast to the caule of her head. Then the two women departed from her, and she kneeling down upon the cushion most resolutely, and without any token or fear of death, she spake aloud this Psalm in Latin, *In Te Domine confido, non confundar in eternam, etc.* Then, groping for the block, she laid down her head, putting her chin over the block with both her hands, which, holding there still, had been cut off had they not been espied. Then lying upon the block most quietly, and stretching out her arms cried, *In manus tuas, Domine*, etc., three or four times. Then, lying very still upon the block, one of the executioners holding her slightly with one of his hands, she endured two strokes of the other executioner with an axe, she making very small noise or none at all, and not stirring any part of her from the place where she lay: and so the executioner cut off her head, saving one little gristle, which being cut asunder, he lift up her head to the view of all the assembly and bade God save the Queen. Then, her dress of lawn falling from off her head, it appeared as grey as one of threescore and ten years old, polled

very short, her face in a moment being so much altered from the form she had when she was alive, as few could remember her by her dead face. Her lips stirred up and down a quarter of an hour after her head was cut off.

•

Anna Wang, a Chinese Christian, was fourteen when she was beheaded by Boxer rebels on July 21, 1900. Her last words: "The door of heaven is open to all. Jesus, Jesus, Jesus."

•

Louis XVI, guillotined on January 21, 1793, said: "I die innocent of all the crimes laid to my charge; I pardon those who have occasioned my death; and I pray to God that the blood you are going to shed may never be visited on France."

•

Sir Walter Raleigh's last words, on October 29, 1618, are uncertain. He either said, "So the heart be right, it is no matter which way the head lieth," or, "Tis a sharp remedy, but a sure cure for all ills."

•

On July 6, 1535, **Sir Thomas More**, Henry VIII's lord chancellor, who had been sentenced to death for treason because he refused to acknowledge Henry as the head of the Church of England, pronounced himself "The King's good servant, but God's first," and then laid his head on the block (see also *You CAN Take It with You*).

•

Hans Scholl, one of the leaders of the White Rose resistance group, was guillotined by the Nazis on February 22, 1943. His last words were "Es lebe die Freiheit" (Long live freedom).

•

American journalist **Daniel Pearl**'s last words, spoken in Karachi and recorded on videotape, February 1, 2002, were "I am Jewish."

•

The mistress of Louis XV, **Madame du Barry**, did not put on a brave face on December 8, 1793: "You are going to hurt me, please don't hurt me, just one more moment, executioner, I beg you." During her time in the Big House, Madame du Barry shared a cell with the equally celebrated courtesan Grace Elliott.

Celebrity Roomies

Grace Elliott escaped unscathed and with tales to tell of her celebrated cell-mate. Here are some other notables who shared quarters when they were starting out and hardly had a quarter to share between them.

- **Gary LeVox** (country singer) and **Jamie Foxx** (actor and Ray Charles impersonator).

- **Al Gore** (Nobel laureate and hectoring environmentalist) and **Tommy Lee Jones** (craggy-faced thespian), at Harvard.

- **Jane Fonda** and **Roger Vadim** shared premises with the eccentric Italian playboy prince and now and again actor **Alessandro "Dado" Ruspoli**.

- **Jude Law** (actor and nanny fancier) and **Ewan McGregor** (actor and enthusiastic participant in filmed nude scenes).

- **Michael Caine** (English actor) and **Vidal Sassoon** (emperor of hair).

- **Daphne Zuniga** (actress, star of *Melrose Place*) and **Meg Ryan** (pixie-like actress somewhat past her pixie prime).

- **Tony Blair** (former British prime minister) and **Charles Falconer**, Baron Falconer of Thoroton (Labour politician).

- Literary luminaries **W.H. Auden**, **Carson McCullers**, **Truman Capote**, **Paul** and **Jane Bowles**; musicians **Benjamin Britten**, **Peter Pears**, and **Colin McPhee**; and burlesque queen and mystery novelist **Gypsy Rose Lee** were all at one time or another resident in a shared house at 7 Middagh Street, in Brooklyn. The linchpin of Middagh Street was the editor and journalist **George Davis**, who claimed he first saw the house in a dream.

- Antipodean actors **Geoffrey Rush** and **Mel Gibson**.

- During the shooting of the 2007 film *Margot at the Wedding*, **Nicole Kidman** shared a house in the Hamptons with her co-stars, **Jack Black** and **Jennifer Jason Leigh**.

- British spies **Kim Philby** and **Guy Burgess** shared a house in Washington, D.C., at 4100 Nebraska Avenue.

Michael Caine

Vidal Sassoon

Riding the Peristaltic Wave

Bears are mentioned in one of my most cherished books, *Two Health Problems: Constipation and Our Civilisation,* by the Scottish naturopath James C. Thomson, published in 1943. The longish subtitle to this monograph more or less sums up the author's thesis: "The Connection between Our Indigestion and Our Indecision; Our Food and Our Behaviour. Advertising Specialists, Pain, Drugs, Enemas . . . With Suggestions for Home Treatment."

There's much to recommend this book, apart from its plentiful, often commonsensical advice on dealing with intestinal sluggishness. For one thing, it contains the most felicitous cautionary phrase ever written in English, albeit one that seems somewhat at odds with every author's desire to have his or her book read and digested by the public: "I take this early opportunity to warn my readers that there can be few occupations more dangerous than reading constipation literature." Dr. Thomson, apparently, had never heard of such vocations as sapper or land-mine sweeper or high-rise window washer. The book's most winning feature, though, is surely the flip-page diagram that runs on the top right-hand side of pages 31 through 109. Leaf quickly through, and you are treated to a rudimentary animation of the "peristaltic wave," a wonderfully subtle portrayal of food (whole grain, no doubt) making a bid for freedom as it is ushered through the bowel. I have derived hours of pleasure from studying this kinetic marvel, which has resulted, perhaps, in a bit more wear on the upper edges of the noted pages than might be ideal.

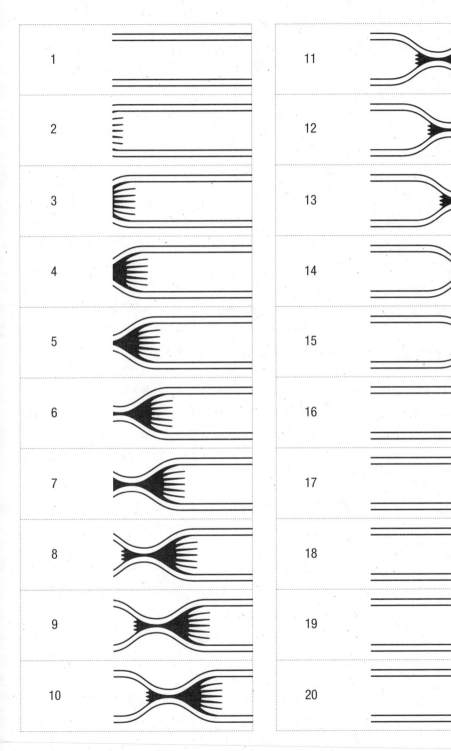

Make your own peristaltic wave flip book. Copy this page, cut, staple in appropriate order, and flip away.
Fun for most of the family!

But we were speaking of bears. Dr. Thomson writes:

According to the folklore of the hunter . . . bears are highly intelligent animals, able to build hide-outs which even an acute observer (if he is not an experienced hunter) cannot detect although he may be standing on top of one. These bears, during the summer, live principally upon fish and grass, but in the late autumn the bear suddenly changes all his feeding habits and for some time he stuffs himself with hay, twigs and pine needles, along with moose and caribou droppings.

But before he begins this strange feast he is said to make a plug of pine needles into a "tappin" or "dottle" with which to plug up his anus. This, the hunters say, is to prevent the escape of any of his store of winter food. Their belief is that when the spring comes the animal wakes up and removes the "tappin" and begins life afresh on salmon, grass, etc., as before.

How does the old song go? "If you go down to the woods today, you're sure of a big surprise"? I imagine this is particularly so if you wander through the forest during the bears' tappin removal festival.

How to Avoid Being Killed by a Bear

After being attacked in a sudden encounter, or perhaps when a charging grizzly is about to contact you, a person should assume a position that will minimize exposure of vital areas and parts of the body where attacks normally focus, such as the face. I recommend the position of facedown, hands behind your neck, with fingers interlocked and legs spread apart for stability should the bear try to roll you over. If the bear does roll you over, keep rolling until your face is again toward the ground. A bear's bite can break or crush the face or neck, but most bear's jaws won't open wide enough to crush the skull of an adult. Another position that has been used to try to minimize injury while playing dead is the fetal position with the hands and arms securing the knees as protection for your face. This position does not protect the neck. Leave your pack on if you have one. The pack should help protect your body.

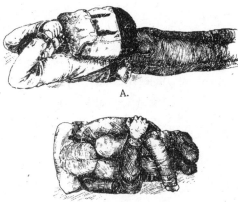

A.

B.

—Stephen Herrero, *Bear Attacks: Their Cause and Avoidance* (1988)

Famous Constipates

Mohandas Gandhi

Constipation and Our Civilisation is frequently cited—most often misnamed as *Constipation and Civilisation*—as one of his favourite books. Possessed of the cloacal fascination that often grips those whose guts are less than co-operative, he was in the habit of inquiring, first thing in the morning, after the state of the bowels of those around him. (See also *Travelling Companions* and *We'll Meet Again—Not!*)

Abraham Lincoln

Lincoln's digestive difficulties have been lavishly documented by many investigators, including John Todd Stuart, Abe's law partner and cousin to Mrs. Lincoln. He told fellow attorney Henry C. Whitney that Lincoln's digestion "was organically defective so that the excreta escaped through the skin pores instead of the bowels." Which must have made him a trying companion in a closed carriage on a long ride.

Sigmund Freud

Ralph Lewin, in *Merde*, says that Freud was a life long sufferer from constipation. Freud, in his *Three Essays on Sexuality*, wrote that there was a sexual component to the retention of fecal matter, and that "few neurotics are to be found without their special scatological practices, ceremonies, and so on, which they carefully keep secret." Old Father William says they really can't be careful enough.

Elvis Presley

Presley suffered, as do many opiate addicts, from severe constipation. The King died, as is well known, while straining on the throne. The weight of his impacted colon has been often and variously reported—forty pounds, fifty pounds, sixty

{ **"Cow" was the code word used by Alice B. Toklas and Gertrude Stein to designate bowel movements.** }

Instructions for better living

How to Keep Your Bowels Open

Those boys who find their digestion sluggish and are troubled with constipation may find the following plan helpful in overcoming the condition. Drink a cool copious draught of water upon rising. Then take some body-bending exercises. Follow this with the sponge bath. Then, if possible, take a walk around the block before breakfast. After school play some favorite game for at least an hour. In the absence of this, take a good hike of three or four miles or a longer bicycle ride. At least twice a week, if possible, enter a gymnasium class and make special emphasis of body-bending exercises.

Have a regular time for going to stool. A good plan is to go just before retiring and immediately upon rising. Go even though you feel no desire to do so. A regular habit may be established by this method. Always respond quickly to any call of nature. Toasted bread and graham bread, fruit and the coarser foods will be found helpful.

"Keep your bowels open" is one of the mottoes every Trail Ranger should know and carry out. By taking the initials of these words, thus, KYBO, you may get a word to remind you of this important function of the body, which may be used without any offense.

pounds. Please. What are we to believe he was packing in there? A Thanksgiving dinner for twenty? And who really needs to know? Stifle the impulse to ask— also about John Wayne, whose innards, post-mortem, have been much parsed.

Napoleon

The Little Emperor ended his days in an agony of intestinal cramping, evidence, some say, of arsenic poisoning.

Martin Luther

In 2004, archeologists, for their own good reasons, poking about Luther's house in Wittenberg, discovered the room that was, apparently, his bog. Here, evidently, Luther spent many hours in forceful exertion and deep contemplation. Luther was, he said, "in cloaca" while working out certain aspects of doctrine, such as the business of salvation springing from faith, rather than through deeds.

Alice B. Toklas

"Cow" was the code word used by Miss Toklas and her companion, Gertrude Stein, to designate bowel movements and other corporeal functions such as orgasm and menstrual flow. To judge by the notes Miss Stein would leave for Miss Toklas, which have been collected in a charming little volume called *Baby Precious Always Shines*, A.B.T. required much encouragement and the stimulation of coffee and cigarettes to produce "sweet cows, smell cows." (Rarely has Old Father William read anything that made him want, simultaneously, to gape and to turn away.)

The King, in a meditative mood, considers his colon.

Edward III

Died in 1377 of a stroke, evidently brought on by severe constipation and, one supposes, the consequent straining.

Catherine the Great

The rumour of her having been done in when the horse with whom she was having carnal relations fell upon her as it was hoisted onto her bed is without foundation. She died of a stroke suffered in her bathroom on November 5, 1796, probably while forcing a bowel movement.

George II

Ditto the above—October 25, 1760—although the consequence of the straining was a rupture of the aorta. What was with these royals and their bowels? Did they not talk to one another?

John Wilmot, Earl of Rochester

As a young man, this swaggering libertine and poetic celebrator of all that was obscene and scatological suffered so badly from constipation that he would go a month between stools.

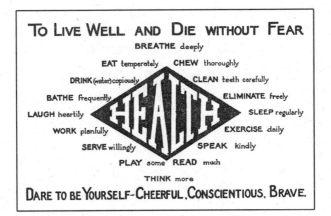

Other Mottoes of Interest

"Y Gwir yn Erbyn y Byd" (Truth against the world).
—*Welsh motto of Frank Lloyd Wright*

"Who the hell ever said it was supposed to be fun, anyway?"
—*Glenn Gould, interviewed in* Horizon Magazine *(1962), named this as the motto that got him through his public performances.*

"Taking Care of Business."
—*Elvis Presley*

"Reason before passion."
—*Pierre Elliott Trudeau*

"Every composer cannot expect to have a worldwide message, but he can reasonably expect to have a special message for his own people."
—*Ralph Vaughan Williams*

"Optimism is true moral courage."
—*Ernest Shackleton*

"Quand même" (which Old Father William translates as, essentially, "Whatever!").
—*Sarah Bernhardt*

"Early to bed, early to rise, work like hell and advertise."
—*Ted Turner*

"Nothing matters."
—*Ambrose Bierce*

"Deeds not words."
—*George Washington*

"Never say Ever and Always."
—*Maria Spiridaki, Miss Greece 2004*

"The freedom of the person ends where it limits the freedom of his fellow
   man."
—*Andrea Denise Muschenborn Charlaix, Miss El Salvador 2004*

"First you feel, then you fall."
—*Vanessa Williams, defrocked Miss America 1984*

"Per scientiam ad justitiam" (Through knowledge to justice).
—*Magnus Hirschfeld, sexologist and gay rights activist*

"Sex heals."
—*Barbara Carrellas, sex educator and pleasure activist*

"Peace through strength."
—*Ronald Reagan*

"New Jersey is open for business."
—*Christine Todd Whitman, governor of New Jersey*

"I will work harder."
—*Boxer, the horse in George Orwell's* Animal Farm

"Saddle your own horse."
—*Connie Reeves, Cowgirl Hall of Fame member, who died after being thrown
   from a horse at the age of 101*

J

Dear Old Father William,
I hope you won't mind that I've taken the liberty of typing up some of your lists. The original manuscripts were beginning to fray something awful. My archival instincts just got the better of me. Do you think you should switch to two-ply?
J.N.

Dear Jane Nurse,
One-ply is kinder to our forests, I think.
O.F.W

Some Good Things to Know about Trees

Grass will grow beneath alder, ash, cypress, elm, plane, and sycamore; but not beneath aspen, beech, chestnut, and fir. Sea-spray does not injure sycamore or tamarisk. Chestnut and olive never warp; larch is most apt to warp. For posts the best woods are yew, oak, and larch; one of the worst is chestnut. For picture-frames, maple, pear, oak, and cherry are excellent. Fleas dislike alder, cedar, myrtle, and yew; hares and rabbits never injure lime bark; moths and spiders avoid cedar; worms never attack juniper. Beech and ash are very subject to attacks of insects. Beech is the favourite tree of dormice, acacia of nightingales. For binding faggots, the best woods are guelder rose, hazel, osier, willow, and mountain ash. Knives and all sorts of instruments may be sharpened on ivy roots, willow, and holly wood, as well as on a hone. Birdlime is made from holly and the guelder rose. Baskets are made of osier, willow, and other wicker and withy shoots; besoms, of birch, tamarisk, heath, etc.; hurdles, of hazel; barrels and tubs, of chestnut and oak; cricket-bats, of willow; fishing-rods, of ash, hazel, and blackthorn; gun-stocks, of maple and walnut; skewers, of elder and skewer wood; the teeth of rakes, of blackthorn, ash, and the twigs called withy. The best woods for turnery are box, alder, beech, sycamore, and pear; for Tunbridge ware, lime; for wood-carving, box, lime, and poplar; for clogs, willow, alder, and beech; for oars, ash. Beech is called the cabinet-makers' wood; oak and elm, the ship-builders'; ash, the wheel-wrights'.

—Ebenezer Cobham Brewer, *Reader's Handbook* (1911)

Trees are devious. They look so inviting to climb, but their bite is worse than their bark. Here are some persons who have tumbled from trees.

•

Trees and trepanning figure in the life of **T. Lobsang Rampa**, into whose skull was bored—according to his own account in *The Third Eye*—a hole that would facilitate clairvoyance. Born Cyril Henry Hoskin, a plumber's son, he claimed that his body was taken over by the spirit of Lobsang Rampa, a Tibetan lama, after he, Cyril, fell from a fir tree in his garden in Thames Ditton, Surrey, while trying to photograph an owl. As Tuesday Lobsang Rampa, Mr. Hoskin went on to write twenty books, including *My Visit to Venus* (the title says it all) and *Living with the Lama,* which was, he claimed, dictated by his Siamese cat, Mrs. Fifi Greywhiskers.

•

On May 24, 2006, **Colin Watson**, an English collector who had often been convicted and fined for stealing wild bird eggs from nests, tried to scale a forty-foot larch in Doncaster, the better to pilfer some sparrow hawk ova. He was three-quarters of the way up—thirty feet, one supposes—when he slipped and fell to his death. He died from a punctured heart and multiple rib fractures. Mr. Watson was sixty-three.

•

A professor of astrophysical sciences at Princeton, and a proponent of the possibility of time travel, **Dr. John Richard Gott III** has said that he became a scientist at the age of three when he became fascinated by gravity after falling out of a tree.

•

On September 14, 1902, the *New York Times* reported the death of **Andrew Reed** and identified him as the hermit of Warren County, New York. Mr. Reed died of blood poisoning, which he contracted several days after falling out of a tree and onto a picket fence. Mr. Reed is not to be confused with Daniel West

(d. 1860), the hermit of Warren County, Tennessee, who lived in the hollow of a riverside poplar tree and was often seen riding through the meadows and vales astride a white steer.

•

On April 27, 2006, Rolling Stones guitarist **Keith Richards** fell from a palm tree in Fiji, sustaining head injuries that required his hospitalization in Auckland. He underwent a craniotomy, i.e., the drilling of small holes in the skull to relieve pressure, an episode and a procedure that interrupted the band's "A Bigger Bang" tour.

•

Martial arts expert and film star **Jackie Chan** was left with a hole in his skull, thimble-sized—the hole, that is, not the skull—when, in 1987, while performing a stunt for the action film *Long xiong hu di* (also known as *Armour of God*), Mr. Chan fell from a tree onto a pile of rocks.

Keith Richards + Jackie Chan + George Bernard Shaw

Gravity at work

•

George Bernard Shaw was a stripling of ninety-four when he fell from a tree he was pruning, fractured his thigh, and never recovered from the injury. He died November 2, 1950.

•

On August 2, 1994, the *Times* (London) reported the story of a woman who was injured when she tumbled, naked, from a tree in a park near Windsor Castle. Evidently, she had been enmeshed in the branches with her boyfriend, though plainly, not securely enough. (In a somewhat related episode, police in Punta Gorda, Florida, summoned a frolicking couple down from a hundred-foot construction crane, in the cab of which the pair had taken naked refuge. When asked what they were doing, unclothed at such a height, they reported that they were photographing the city skyline.)

·

The celebrated Hungarian playwright and novelist **Ödön von Horváth** ended his days not by falling from a tree but after being fallen upon by one. He was taken out in Paris on June 1, 1938, when he was struck by a branch of a chestnut tree wrested loose from its trunk during a rain storm. Ironically, this was also the date that Superman—who might have intervened in such a situation, by swooping out of the sky or by incinerating the branch with his laser-beam eyes—appeared in the first issue of *Action* comics.

Hungarian playwright crushed, but not by bad review.

In January 2000, right-handed pitcher **Carlton Loewer**, of the San Diego Padres, suffered a severe compound fracture to his leg when he fell from a tree while hunting near his home in Louisiana. Kevin Towers, the team's general manager, told the *Denver Post,* "Carlton had to apply a tourniquet to his calf to stop the bleeding. He had to crawl some 700 yards through a swamp to reach his three wheeler and then ride 5 miles for help." Mercy!

•

Katherine FitzGerald, Countess of Desmond, who exited this life in 1604, and who danced in her youth with Richard III, whom she described as "the straightest and properest man she ever saw," died after falling out of a tree: either a nut tree or a cherry tree, depending on the source. Sir William Temple vouched for the former when he wrote, "She must needs climb a tree to gather nuts, so, falling down, she hurt her thigh, which brought a fever and her death." Her age is reliably reported to have been 140.

•

Daryl Hatten, a well-known mountain climber from Victoria, B.C., died on August 21, 2004, when he fell sixty feet from an arbutus tree onto the rocky ground below. He was being paid seventy-five dollars to rescue a cat.

One also notes that on May 17, 2000, the Board of County Commissioners of Hillsborough County, Florida, established the Lonnie Lea Napier Good Neighbor Award, in honour of—who else?—**Lonnie Lea Napier**, who, like Mr. Hatten, died after falling from a tree while trying to rescue a neighbour's cat. One wonders why the commissioners would encourage such behaviour.

J

Dear Old Father William,

I'm making headway with the typing of the lists. I don't mean to meddle in their compilation or to extend my involvement beyond that of amanuensis and caterer, but I can't stop myself from mentioning that in Gabriel Garcia Márquez's Love in the Time of Cholera, Dr. Juvenal Urbino has a parrot who can quote the gospel according to St. Matthew and sing French cabaret songs. Dr. Urbino dies when he falls from a mango tree that he had climbed in order to coax down the miraculous bird.

Of course, when I say "typing up your lists" I mean that I'm "inputting the data," as they say. They live in my computer, so no trees have been sacrificed!

J.N.

Polly Math:
A Calculation of Parrots

Harold Robbins, the Gabriel García Márquez of pulp fiction and the author of such bestsellers as *The Carpetbaggers,* was inclined to bolster his own myth by larding it with stories that were improbable but widely circulated. He put it about, for instance, that his first wife was a Chinese dancer—she was not—who, on their wedding day, was bitten by a parrot—no such grim bird hovered near the altar—and died of psittacosis. She didn't.

•

Steve Irwin, the Australian adventurer known as the Crocodile Hunter who came to grief in the embrace of a stingray on September 4, 2006, admitted to being leery of parrots, if not formally phobic.

•

Adelina Patti, the Spanish-born soprano who was, next to Jenny Lind, probably the greatest diva of the nineteenth century—and also the great-great-aunt of the Broadway star Patti LuPone—had a parrot named Ben Butler, whom she trained to shriek, "Cash, cash!" whenever her manager walked into the room. Patti was one of Verdi's favourite singers and, on one occasion, she sang Rosina's famous aria from *The Barber of Seville,* "Una voce poco fa," for the opera's composer, **Gioachino Rossini** (see *Haste and Waste*). She gussied the tune up with many ornaments, provoking Rossini to say, "That's lovely. Who wrote it?" Rossini

Patti's parrot performs his preferred party trick.

was also a parrot fancier and dedicated one of his later piano pieces to his "petite parruche."

•

The *New York Times*, in September 1906, reported that a Mexican parrot named Dewey, the "pride of City Marshal **David Kraushaar**," was "in the icebox waiting for such immortality as a taxidermist can give him. He could yell louder than all the peddlers of the east side and swear as skillfully as any Delancey Street patrolman." The bird, which was known for its ability to sing "The Star-Spangled Banner," had pined away while awaiting the return of Mrs. Kraushaar from a seven-week vacation. When she at last came home, reported the *Times*, "the bird had its head under its wing. It was on the bottom of the cage, too weak to stand on the perch. Mrs. Kraushaar spoke to her pet, calling him by name. He lifted his head, opened one eye, said, 'Oh, mamma,'... and fell back dead. It was too late to find a taxidermist last night and that's why Dewey was placed in the icebox."

•

Parrots and cold also figure in a story told by **Ignacy Paderewski**, the celebrated pianist and prime minister of Poland, in his memoir. While on a concert tour of Australia in 1927, he and his wife acquired a whole flock of "thirty or forty" parrots, "of all kinds, all ages, all sizes, and all colors. With a multitude of cages we traveled through Australia and New Zealand to San Francisco." Chief among the birds was Cockey Roberts who, according to Paderewski, would come into the room where his owner was practising, perch upon the pianist's pedal foot, and say, "Oh, Lord, how beautiful! How beautiful." Cockey Roberts's voice was hard to bear, and after one memorable shriek left the sonically sensitive Paderewski unnerved for a whole day, the parrot was sent to live with the poultry. He died of cold in the henhouse, in Morges, Switzerland. Paderewski wrote,

> I was then in New York, and I remember well that the whole of one night I dreamed of Cocky [sic] Roberts. I dreamed about him and saw him,

and I heard his funny, shrill, angry little voice calling me and it did not seem so unpleasant to me in my dreams. And somehow, I knew then that Cocky Roberts was dead and there was a very empty little place in my heart. Ten days afterwards we received the news from Morges that poor Cockey Roberts was no more.

•

The great nineteenth-century piano virtuoso **Elie-Miriam Delaborde** fled France and the ravages of the Franco-Prussian war for England with a retinue of 121 parrots and cockatoos. He came by his parrotophilia and his pianistic chops honestly; he was the student and illegitimate son of **Charles-Valentin Alkan**, a reclusive composer of famously finger-fracturing music, as well as the novelty number "Funeral March for a Dead Parrot." The text consists of the French equivalent of "Polly want a cracker?": *As-tu déjeuné, Jaco?*

•

Jaco was **Joseph Haydn**'s parrot. He outlived his owner and was listed last among the effects of the composer when they went to auction: "No. 614: A living parrot. From the breed of teachable Jacos, the size of a pigeon, grey with a red tail. Since according to all natural historians parrots attain a high age of about 100 years this one is still young. Herr Haydn bought him 19 years ago, not fully grown, in London, for a high price, and taught him himself. Lives, as is customary, in a metal cage."

•

Queen Victoria's African Grey, Coco, sang "God Save the Queen" when she entered the room. Coco is also the name of a parrot in the Greek city of Patras who, in 2006, was the object of a legalistic donnybrook when he—or rather, his owner, **Lambros Micholopolous**—was fined €444 because his outdoor perch was taking up part of a parking spot. The American painter **Mary Cassatt** had a parrot called Coco to whom Edgar Degas wrote an appreciative

{ **A passage from Beethoven's Fifth Symphony was the last mastered by Papo, Richard Wagner's parrot.** }

sonnet. Coco is the name of the parrot who dies a fiery death in the **Jean Rhys** novel *The Wide Sargasso Sea,* and **Prince Leopold of Belgium**'s parrot also answered to Coco.

Charlotte was the name of **George V**'s parrot, who was his constant companion, and who accompanied the King's casket on the funeral train when he died in 1936. **Charlotte Mew,** the eccentric English lesbian poet—who took her life by drinking Lysol—had an inherited, man-hating, manuscript-chewing parrot called Baby. In 1816, **Charlotte, Princess of Wales**, also had a parrot forced on her when she married Leopold, Prince of the Belgians, owner of Coco (above). The two of them—Charlotte and Coco, that is—would sometimes sing duets.

In 1817, Charlotte took delivery of a Broadwood piano in a satin and rosewood case, decorated with ormolu. It was identical to the piano delivered in that same year to Ludwig van Beethoven. A passage from Beethoven's Fifth Symphony was the last passage mastered by Papo, **Richard Wagner**'s parrot, before the bird expired. Wagner expressed his grief at this loss in a letter to a friend: "Ah, if I could say to you what has died for me in this devoted creature! It matters nothing to me whether I am laughed at for this."

•

Charlie was allegedly the name of **Winston Churchill**'s parrot, who, according to stories widely circulated in the early years of the twenty-first century, was still alive and prospering and repeating ad nauseam the phrase Churchill taught him: "Fuck Hitler and fuck the Nazis." Sir Winston's daughter, Lady Soames, DBE, did her best to cauterize the scurrilous flow with this letter to a publication of record:

> My father never owned a Macaw in the 1930s or at any other time as far as I am aware. He did own an African Grey Parrot in the mid to late Thirties. I do not know how he acquired it—it may well be as stated in the offending piece. I cannot remember the parrot's name; it was quite disagreeable and frequently bit those who tried to curry favour with it

Charlotte, Princess of Wales, and her parrot, Coco, would sometimes sing duets.

(including WSC). The parrot lived in a large cage in the dining room at Chartwell. The bird did not spend the war at my father's side; when the family removed from Chartwell to London in September/October 1939 I have the impression the parrot had a good home found for it.

•

Somewhat specious sounding is the story reported in several English newspapers and wire services in 2006 about a parrot called Ziggy, who, it is said, began using the phrase "I love you, Gary," thus revealing to his owner the sordid truth of a dalliance between the gentleman's girlfriend and said Gary. Ziggy declined to quit invoking the name of Gary when the relationship ended—which it did jolly quickly—and had to be handed on to a new owner.

J

Dear Old Father William,

I know that I promised not to interfere, but there's an addictive quality to this business, once you get going, so I can't stop myself from pointing out, vis-à-vis the composer Alkan and his funeral march for the dead parrot—is that where the Monty Python team got the idea for their famous sketch?—an opera by Jacques Offenbach called Vert-Vert. It's not much performed, perhaps because the Vert-Vert of the title is a parrot, a mascot at a girl's school who has died of constipation, which is also of interest to you, now that I think of it. The action takes place at the bird's funeral.

    Furthermore—and after this I do promise that I'll shut up—you might want to add to your list of persons who tumbled from trees the name Franco De Benedetto. In May

J

2004, he wound up in hospital after he came a-cropper while trying to cut down an art work installed in a tree in Milan by Maurizio Cattelan. The offending work was plastic figures of three hanging children. Signor De Benedetto suffered multiple fractures and was later sentenced to three months in jail for defacing a work of art. A cautionary tale!

J.N.

Other Awful Scandals Wrought by Artful Vandals

Dror Feiler

In January 2004, in Stockholm, Dror Feiler's installation *Snow White and the Madness of Truth* was the object of an attack by Zvi Mazel, the Israeli ambassador to Sweden. Mr. Mazel threw a spotlight at the piece, a small ship sailing in a pool of blood and bearing a photograph of suicide bomber Hanadi Jaradat, who killed herself and twenty-one others in Haifa. Mr. Mazel's actions were defended by then prime minister Ariel Sharon.

Michelangelo

In September 1991, Piero Camata said he was "jealous of Michelangelo" and hammered off the tip of one toe of *David*. Laszlo Toth was more loquacious when he explained why he administered fifteen hammer blows to the *Pietà* on May 21, 1972, in St. Peter's Basilica: "Today is my 33rd birthday, the day when Christ died. For that reason, I smashed the *Pietà* today. I did it because the mother of God does not exist. I am Christ. I am Michelangelo. I have reached the age of Christ and now I can die. Certainly you can kill me; go ahead and kill me; but I am Jesus Christ and if you kill me I am going straight to heaven."

Jean Auguste Dominique Ingres

Ingres's *The Sistine Chapel* came under attack in the Louvre in 1907, when Valentine Contrel used scissors to slash the painting. Contrel explained that she was hungry, cold, and unemployed, and simply wanted to get arrested. Hugo Unzaga Villegas took a page from her book and, in order to be admitted to a nice warm jail, threw a stone at the *Mona Lisa* in 1956.

Jacob Epstein

Epstein's art deco monument to Oscar Wilde (see also *Died in a Hotel*), which marks the writer's Parisian burial place in Père Lachaise Cemetery, and which represents a stylized naked angel, was emasculated by persons unknown. The playwright's private parts are popularly thought to have been removed, with a hammer, by outraged English tourists.

Similarly, throughout 1985, a vandal systematically removed the noses from eighty stone statues in the Villa Borghese in Rome. The culprit, when finally apprehended, was found with a bag full of stone appendages. He was carrying a note in which he claimed to be a UFO.

Barnett Newman

Gerard Jan van Bladeren twice attacked paintings by Barnett Newman. In 1986, in Amsterdam's Stedelijk Museum, he had at *Who's Afraid of Red, Yellow, and Blue III* with a Stanley knife. In the same museum, in 1997, van Bladeren took a knife to *Cathedra*.

Cy Twombly

In 2007, Rindy Sam, a French artist, planted a lipstick kiss on a pure white Cy Twombly painting, unnamed, which was part of an exhibition at the Collection Lambert in Avignon. "Twombly left this white for me," she said, by way of explaining the smooch. The painting was valued at two million dollars. Sam, who said at her trial that it was an act of love, was sentenced to serve one hundred hours of community service. The lipstick, by the way, was Lovely Rouge, by Bourjois.

Jo Baer

In 1977, in Oxford, at the Museum of Modern Art, Ruth van Herpen thought to wake with a kiss a white monochrome canvas by the American artist Jo Baer. At her trial, van Herpen said she found the painting cold, and wanted to "cheer it up." Similarly, in 1912, a young woman applied a bit of rouge to a François Boucher portrait in the Louvre, concerned that the subject was "lacking colour."

{ **A vandal systematically removed the noses from eighty stone statues in the Villa Borghese.** }

Pablo Picasso

In 1974, Tony Shafrazi, who went on to run a successful gallery in New York, inscribed *Guernica* with the phrase "KILL LIES ALL."

Edvard Eriksen

Eriksen created the statue of the Little Mermaid perched on the rock at the entrance to Copenhagen harbour. The tribute to Hans Christian Andersen has been defaced on numerous occasions: covered in paint, decapitated, and blown off her rock with explosives.

Marcel Duchamp

Duchamp, who once advised "use a Rembrandt as an ironing board," would probably not have minded anything that has happened to his artworks. On May 21, 2000, Yuan Cai and Jian Jun Xi, two Chinese artists describing themselves as "heroes ahead of our time," urinated on Duchamp's *Fountain* (a piece of "found art" consisting of an actual urinal), and later announced: "The urinal is there, it's an invitation. As Duchamp said himself, it's the artist's choice. He chooses what is art. We just added to it."

Duchamp's urinal had already been the object of an inundation in 1993, though at the time nobody seemed exactly sure whether the liquid the performance artist Pierre Pinoncelli poured on it in Nîmes was urine or tea (it could, of course, have been one, then the other). The sixty-nine-year-old Pinoncelli was arrested, imprisoned, and ordered to pay 250,000 francs to an insurance company, 16,336 francs for repairs, and 10,000 francs in costs. In addition, the

Ministry of Culture demanded 20,000 francs. In January 2006, Pinoncelli was fined the equivalent of $262,000 for having once again had his way with *Fountain*. This time he had managed to chip at it with a hammer and scrawl the word "Dada" across it.

Pinoncelli's devotion to such shenanigans is extraordinary. In 1969, at the opening of a Chagall exhibition in Nice, he had attacked André Malraux (then minister of culture) with a paint-filled water pistol, and in 2002, he chopped off his little finger during an arts festival in Colombia (in apparent solidarity with kidnapped presidential candidate Ingrid Betancourt).

Art Strikes Back

Robert Smithson, the celebrated earthworks artist, was killed when the plane from which he was surveying the site for a sculpture to be called *Amarillo Ramp* crashed on July 20, 1973.

•

Ambroise Vollard, the art dealer who represented Picasso and Matisse among many others, died in a car crash on July 22, 1939, at the age of seventy-three. It is said he was struck in the head by a small bronze sculpture by Maillol that he kept in his car, a Talbot convertible. It is also said that the fatal missile was the casserole containing the cassoulet he was taking to his neighbour's for lunch.

•

Luis Jimenez, a well-known sculptor from New Mexico, was killed in 2006 when part of a giant horse he was creating for the Denver airport swung out of control while it was being hoisted and fell on him, severing an artery in his leg.

•

Harvey Fite spent thirty-eight years working on *Opus 40,* a sculpted environment chiselled out of a bluestone quarry in the upstate New York township of Saugerties. He lived and worked alone, using leverage methods familiar to pyramid builders to manipulate and move enormous tonnages of stone. He died in 1976, dashed to death on the hard edges of his own creation when his lawnmower became stuck in gear and drove over the edge of the quarry.

•

James Wells Champney, a popular American painter of the late nineteenth century, eager to develop some photographic plates and in a hurry to reach the eighth floor of the building that housed the Camera Club, was killed falling down an elevator shaft. When the lift stalled between the fourth and fifth floors, he ignored the advice of the elevator boy, jimmied the door, swung himself out on the cables, and fell.

•

In 1998, **Laura Roberts**, aged five, was killed in Torremolinos, Spain, when a six-foot statue of a goddess toppled on her. And in May 1993, a four-year-old boy visiting his grandmother at a spiritual retreat in Baltimore was killed when a statue of the Virgin Mary fell on him. In 2000, in Ireland, a boy who was severely injured by a falling statue of the Virgin received £1.1 million. In Waterville, Maine, in 1996, a man killed two nuns using a statue of the Virgin Mary as a weapon.

Dear Old Father William,

Re: Polly Math. I showed this to my grandson, who wants me to tell you that he thinks it should be called "The Last Time I Saw Parrots." There may be hope for the lad. He also tells me that in Australian slang, loin-hugging briefs are known as "budgie smugglers." I wonder if his parents should be paying closer attention to his website use.

By the way, I've been meaning to tell you, one of the members of my opera club is in the publishing industry. I happened to mention your list-making enterprise and she wondered if she could take a look at the collection so far. Do I have your permission?

J.N.

The Secrets of Seven

A budgie, smuggled or otherwise, wouldn't last long at Dude Cottage, where there are seven cats in residence, each one more revolting than the last. Their names reflect their personal liabilities, in case you were wondering: Birdbreath Bertie and Daggy Uncle Bunny, Major General Chunder Puss and Goop-Eye Gomer, Dicky the Drooler and Ol' Man Fartsalot. Last—and, in a quantitative way, least—is Tripod Ted, whose disability renders the sum of their legs twenty-seven; a pity, because were they fully limbed, I could rent them out to *Sesame Street,* or some such high-flying agency, as a four times table didactic aid and they could earn their considerable keep.

Ted is a creature of resolute, poisonous nastiness. This was so when he was conventionally endowed in the leg department, and amputation did nothing to waken in his heart the latent sweetness of the suffering martyr. I suspect the coyote who began Ted's dismantling suffered such a case of gastritis from the one drumstick he was able to wrest free that "cat" was forevermore stricken from his diet.

Seven is a fine number for a collective if it refers to the hills of Rome or the wonders of the world or the years required to graduate from Hogwarts; it's a suitable tally for deadly sins, or for seas to sail, or for the symphonies of Sibelius. Seven is groovy if you're totting up the joys of Mary. But when seven's the count of the clowder of cats in your cottage, you've got more than alliteration. You've got trouble, my friend: trouble and one hell of a lot of dander.

Here are some other clusters of seven, most of them more savoury than the Dude brood.

The Group of Seven
The members of this cluster of iconic Canadian landscape painters, in alphabetical order, are Franklin Carmichael, Lawren Harris, A.Y. Jackson, Frank Johnston, Arthur Lismer, J.E.H. MacDonald, and Frederick Varley.

{ **Dopey was the only one of the seven dwarves who was clean shaven.** }

Liz's Legion

A group named formally for the first time here, Elizabeth Taylor's seven hus-
bands, in order of acquisition, were Conrad (Nicky) Hilton, Michael Wilding,
Michael Todd, Eddie Fisher, Richard Burton (twice), John Warner, and Larry
Fortensky.

The Secret Seven

The young investigators whose adventures were recounted by Enid Blyton in
fifteen novels published between 1949 and 1963 are Peter, Janet, Jack, Colin,
George, Pam, and Barbara. Scamper, the spaniel, was not formally a part of the
agency. Their meetings were held in a garden shed (see also *Shedding Season*).

The Seven Sages of the Bamboo Grove

Chinese Taoist poets and musicians, they gathered in a bamboo grove to swill
ale, advocate the simple pleasures of rustic living, and criticize the corrupt
ways of the Imperial Court. The members were Xi Kang, Liu Ling, Ruan Ji,
Ruan Xian, Xiang Xiu, Wang Rong, and Shan Tao. In his book *Homosexuality
and Civilization*, Louis Crompton writes of the relationship between Xi Kang
and Ruan Ji, whose connection was, apparently, "stronger than metal and fra-
grant as orchids."

La Pléiade

Named for the seven-member star cluster, the members of this group of
Renaissance poets, philosophers, and French-language advocates were Pierre
de Ronsard, Joachim du Bellay, Rémy Belleau, Étienne Jodelle, Pontus de Tyard,
Jean-Antoine de Baïf, and the humanist scholar Jean Dorat.

Copeland's Septet

Discovered by Ralph Copeland, the Astronomer Royal of Scotland, in 1874, these
seven major galaxies in the constellation Leo are some 480 million light-years
away, about 8°NW of Denebola. Their New Galaxy Catalogue (NGC) numbers
are 3745, 3746, 3748, 3750, 3751, 3753, and 3754. Mr. Copeland observed the septet
using the seventy-two-inch "Leviathan of Parsonstown" at Birr Castle.

Seven-Part Mnemonics

The Seven Hills of Rome

Queen	**Q**uirinal
Victoria	**V**iminal
Eyes	**E**squiline
Caesar's	**C**aelian
Awfully	**A**ventine
Painful	**P**alatine
Corns	**C**apitoline

The Countries of Central America

Big	**B**elize
Gorillas	**G**uatemala
Eat	**E**l Salvador
Hotdogs	**H**onduras
Not	**N**icaragua
Cold	**C**osta Rica
Pizza	**P**anama.

The Seven Components of the Bowel

Dow	**D**uodenum
Jones	**J**ejunum
Industrial	**I**leum
Average	**A**ppendix
Closing	**C**olon
Stock	**S**igmoid
Report	**R**ectum

Seven Manners of Articulation

Stop	**S**top
Fooling	**F**ricative
Around	**A**ffricate
Now	**N**asal
Learn	**L**iquid
Good	**G**lide
Voicing	**V**owel

The Seven Layers of the Scrotum

Some	**S**kin
Damn	**D**artos fascia
Englishman	**E**xternal spermatic fascia
Called	**C**remaster
It	**I**nternal spermatic fascia
The	**T**unica vaginalis
Testis	**T**estis

188

The Seven Samurai

The warriors in the 1954 Akira Kurosawa film—the inspiration for the 1960 John Sturges classic of vigilante justice, *The Magnificent Seven*—are Kambei Shimada, Katsushirō Okamoto, Gorōbei Katayama, Shichirōji, Kyuzō, Heihachi Hayashida, and Kikuchiyo.

The Gang of Seven

This group of Republican U.S representatives, elected in 1990, loudly condemned the House banking scandal and the congressional post office scandal. They also criticized congressional perks such as subsidies for the Capitol barbershop and Senate restaurant. The seven representatives were John Boehner, John Doolittle, Scott Klug, Jim Nussle, Frank Riggs, Charles H. Taylor, and Rick Santorum.

Six Actors, Seven Dwarves

Old Father William, when he feels the need to test his memory and be sure that it hasn't been totally trampled by the tireless tread of time, will sometimes see if he can call to mind the names of the seven dwarves in *Snow White*; on a very fine day, I can also name the actors who provided their voices.

Bashful: Scotty Mattraw

His first screen appearance was as a eunuch in the 1924 Douglas Fairbanks vehicle *The Thief of Baghdad*, which also featured Anna May Wong as a Mongol slave.

Grumpy and Sleepy: Pinto Colvig

Colvig had a long and distinguished career in comedy. In 1947, he became the first Bozo the Clown. An inveterate, if repentant, smoker, he was an early advocate of warning labels on cigarette packs. He died of lung cancer on October 3, 1967.

Doc: Roy Atwell

The author of "Some Little Bug Is Going to Find You," a really remarkable bit of versified invention about pathogens in the early twentieth century, and one of Old Father William's poetic touchstones:

Eating lobster cooked or plain is only flirting with ptomaine
And an oyster often has a lot to say
Those clams they put in chowder make the angels sing the louder
For they know that they'll be with you right away.
(see also *Laid Low by a Bivalve*).

Atwell played many bit parts in many movies. He followed up *Snow White* with a role in *Honolulu* as "Bearded Man on Ship."

Sneezy: Billy Gilbert

As a vaudevillian, he developed a sneezing routine that made him a dead cert for this role.

Happy: Otis Harlan

Harlan was born in Zanesville, Ohio (Zane Grey was a descendant of the town's founding father). It was Harlan who first performed the Irving Berlin classic "Alexander's Ragtime Band," on the vaudeville stage in 1911. A year later, that song was among the tunes played by the brave band aboard the *Titanic* while the ship foundered and sank. The Ethel Merman disco version of the song, from her ill-advised album of 1979, would be enough to make anyone book passage on the *Titanic,* as long its sinking were assured.

Dopey: Eddie Collins

Collins performed opposite Ethel Merman in the film version of *Alexander's Ragtime Band* (1938) and had the distinction of "playing" the dog in *The Blue Bird,* Shirley Temple's first-ever box office flop (1940). Dopey was the only one of the seven dwarves who was clean shaven.

Instructions for better living

HOW TO SHARPEN A RAZOR

A sealskin strop, having a smooth, pliable surface, gives the best edge; and if the razor be dipped into hot water before stropping, the metal is toughened and better fitted for the production of the requisite keen edge. The preliminary immersion in water is a vital factor, since razors possess a finer temper than ordinary cutting tools, and are proportionately brittle. It is also expedient that the strop-surface should be preserved from the settling thereon of dust particles, the presence of which, if of a gritty nature, may break the delicate edge of the tool. It is important to remember that the edge of a razor, being obviously of a much finer character, owing to the nature of its work, than other cutting tools, must receive special attention, and by taking to heart the foregoing simple rules many of the difficulties presently experienced may be overcome.

—Professor McWilliam, address to the Sheffield Society of Engineers and Metallurgists on "The Care of a Razor," as reported in *Chambers's Journal* (1888)

Shaves Too Close for Comfort

Old Father William would like to point out that his inclusion of the foregoing instructions in the present volume in no way implies advocacy of the procedures they describe. Get a sealskin strop if you want to, friend, and make the edge of your blade as keen as ever you can. But don't come crying to me if there are consequences that require more staunching than your average styptic pencil can bring to bear. As the amplitude of his beard attests, it's been a great many years since Old Father William's facial flesh has known the whetted caress of a sharpened scythe.

He would like to point out that a later *Chambers's Journal,* which publication contained the instructions for sharpening a razor, also included the following report, headlined "Anthrax Infection in Shaving Brushes," which reads, in part,

> One would hardly expect to find danger lurking in shaving-brushes, yet such is the case. . . . The instances of anthrax infection traceable to shaving-brushes numbered sixty-five in the past two years (nineteen civilians and forty-six soldiers). An investigation into several of these cases revealed the fact that the infected shaving-brushes, although purchased at different shops, were all made in the same factory. Further inquiries proved that some of the horsehair used was imported from China as "goat's hair," which is not compulsorily disinfected, as is foreign horsehair. . . . Infection was also traced to brushes made in Japan, the United States, and Canada.

Were Old Father William inclined to travel, he would go to Washington's Smithsonian Institution to see the seventeen-and-a-half-foot beard that once belonged to Hans Langseth, a North Dakotan of Norwegian descent, who left North Dakota for Heaven in 1927. Given the potentially dire outcomes of shaving, Hans was perhaps well advised to eschew the razor.

Albert Anastasia, mobster and leading executioner of the syndicate Murder, Inc., was gunned down in the barber shop of the Park Sheraton Hotel on October 25, 1957. **Johnny Torio**, a.k.a. "The Brain," a leading mobster and associate of Al Capone, died more peacefully of a heart attack in a barber's chair on April 16, 1957.

•

John Buchan, **Lord Tweedsmuir**, governor general of Canada and author of some eighty books including *The Thirty-Nine Steps*, had a stroke while shaving on February 6, 1940, fell, struck his head, and died five days later.

•

On June 29, 2006, while shaving, **David Hasselhoff**, star of the television series *Baywatch* and a serial abuser of moisturizers, had a violent collision with either a Tiffany lamp or a glass shelf—reports vary— in the gym of the Sanderson Hotel, London. The resultant shards sliced tendons and arteries in his arm. He was treated at St. Thomas' Hospital and, unfortunately, released.

•

George Edward Stanhope Molyneux Herbert, the fifth earl of Carnarvon and the money behind Howard Carter's discovery of the tomb of Tutankhamun, died of an erysipelas infection caused when he nicked a mosquito bite while shaving, in Cairo, on April 5, 1923. It's reported that, at the moment of his death, the Egyptian capital was plunged into darkness and his dog, back home in England, howled and keeled over dead.

•

John Hodiak, the American star of *Lifeboat* and *A Bell for Adano,* had a heart attack while shaving in his parents' home in Tarzana, California, and died on October 19, 1955.

•

John Thoreau, elder brother of Henry, cut his finger while shaving and died five days later of lockjaw on January 11, 1842. He was twenty-six. In 1928, in Winnipeg, three thousand disappointed concertgoers were unable to hear **Fritz Kreisler** who had, Thoreau-like, cut his finger while shaving.

•

Ferruccio Busoni, the virtuoso pianist and composer (1866–1924) was taken as a little boy to see **Franz Liszt** perform. He was unimpressed with the great man's playing, and learned only years later that Liszt had been holding back on the keyboard pyrotechnics because he had cut his finger while shaving.

•

Max Baer, the heavyweight boxing champ, was shaving in his hotel room on November 21, 1959, when he suffered a fatal heart attack (see also *Died at Fifty, Died in a Hotel*).

•

King Charles II was stricken, while shaving, with an apoplectic fit. Naturally, given his station, no effort was spared to ease his discomfort and hasten a cure. His chief physician, Sir Charles Scarburgh, left a description of the various palliatives that were brought to bear. There was an enema that used antimony, sacred bitters, rock salt, mallow leaves, violet, beetroot, camomile flowers, fennel seed, linseed, cinnamon, cardamom seed, saffron, cochineal, and aloes. His scalp was shaved and blistered. He received a sneezing powder of hellebore root, and was also administered a vast bevy of purgatives concocted of barley water, liquorice, sweet almonds, white wine, absinthe, anise seed, and extracts of thistles, rue, mint, and angelica. A poultice of burgundy pitch and pigeon was laid on his feet, and he was administered gentian root, nutmeg, quinine, and cloves and forty drops of an extract made from a human skull. After all that, he popped off anyway. At least he was fresh faced.

•

Finally, on November 14, 1895, the *New York Times* reported the deaths by hanging of three men executed for murder. They had crammed the body of **Fillipo Caruso**, a fruit peddler, into a quite small trunk and shipped it to Pittsburgh, where, for predictable olfactory reasons, it attracted a certain amount of attention in the station. The crime was committed on April 30. Caruso was invited into a house where he found the three men shaving each other. Asked if he, too, wanted a treatment, he acceded and sat down: "Lather was spread over his face, but before the razor was applied the three men, Azari, Silvestri, and Gelardi, gently placed a stout, thin rope over his throat, and, wrapping it quickly around, pulled it tight. Death soon followed, and no time was lost packing the body in the trunk and shipping it."

Why the trio wanted Caruso out of the way is not disclosed in the report, but great attention is paid to the hanging. For Silvestri and Gelardi, it was a case of over and out; Azari was not so lucky. "The noose slipped when the rope stretched, and the knot lodged under his chin. He drew up his legs, shudders ran through his frame, and his convulsions were terrible to see. . . . For four minutes the twitching lasted, while the gasps, longer intervals ensuing between each, did not cease until five and a half minutes had elapsed. It was seven minutes before the pulse ceased to beat."

Smallest Room, Biggest Risk

Most shaving, unless it's done by a professional in a shop or salon, takes place in the bathroom, to which room Old Father William long ago retired, never to re-emerge. Lest anyone think that part of my rationale in choosing the lav as my site of hermitage has to do with sidestepping disaster, let me remind you of the oft-cited statistic that the bathroom is the most hazardous place in the house. In fact, I am living very much on the edge.

•

On June 17, 1915, in the coastal resort of Cape May, New Jersey, the by-then ex-president **William Howard Taft** gave a moistly telling demonstration of Archimedean principles. Taft—rhymes with raft—was there to address the Pennsylvania Bankers' Association. The financiers were concerned when their vaunted guest—a man of vast flesh, tipping the scales at 332 pounds—didn't appear at the appointed time; they were the more concerned when a wet spot appeared in the ceiling above them, followed by a steady dripping. Taft proved to be the source of the flow. He had fallen asleep in the tub and didn't notice that he was displacing a tidal flow of warm and soapy water. Much merriment ensued.

Taft once got stuck in the White House bathtub and had a special fixture installed to circumvent future embarrassment: it was seven feet long and forty-one inches wide. Taft was the last president to have cows grazing the lawns of the White House. Paulin was the name of the final cow accorded that ruminative honour.

•

On December 10, 1968, **Thomas Merton**, the Trappist monk and popular author of such contemplative texts as *The Seven Storey Mountain,* stepped from his bath in Bangkok, touched an inadequately grounded electric fan, and was electrocuted.

> Statistics show that the bathroom is
> the most hazardous room in the house.

•

Agamemnon, big-time Greek and one of the fabled principals of the Trojan wars, was murdered in his bath by his wife, Clytemnestra. Similarly, on July 13, 1793, **Jean-Paul Marat**, one of the architects of the French Revolution, and the host to a painful skin condition that was somewhat mitigated by immersion in water, was murdered in his bath by Charlotte Corday. The tub, minus its famous tenant, is on display in the Musée Grévin in Paris.

•

Paul Morphy, an American chess prodigy thought by many historians of the game to have been among its most brilliant players, retired from the game at the age of twenty-one and lived out the rest of his life (twenty-six years) as a mostly non-practising lawyer and semi-recluse in New Orleans. Able from earliest childhood to recite from memory the whole Civil Code of Louisiana, he was apparently given to such eccentricities as arranging women's shoes in a semi-circle in his room and pacing the porch while reciting the phrase, "Il plantera la bannière de Castille sur les murs de Madrid, au cri de Ville gagnée, et le petit roi s'en ira tout penaud" (that is, "He will plant the banner of Castile on the walls of Madrid with the cry, The city is conquered and the little king will have to go"). On July 10, 1884, he took a long walk in hot weather, then immersed himself in a cold bath, and died.

•

Mark Twain's daughter, **Jean Clemens**, died in the bath on Christmas Eve 1909, after an epileptic seizure.

•

On October 5, 1898, the *New York Times* reported the death, by drowning in the bathtub, of the **Hon. William Strutt**, aged twenty-three, son and heir to Baron Belper of Kingston Hall, Derby, England, and nephew of the Earl of Dunford, a "Scotch peer" who was a lord-in-waiting to Queen Victoria. What Mr. Strutt was doing at the West End Hotel in St. Louis, where the death occurred, was not disclosed.

•

The bathroom has long been a favourite site of expiry for showbiz types, especially when drugs are involved. The case of Elvis has already been noted (see *Famous Constipates*); here are a few other examples:

- On April 14, 1983, **Peter Farndon**, the bassist with the Pretenders, died in his bath after overdosing on heroin.
- On July 3, 1971, **Jim Morrison**, the main knob of the Doors, was found dead in his bathtub, in Paris. The cause of his death, and the circumstances around it, are favoured fodder for conspiracy theorists worldwide.
- On June 22, 1969, **Judy Garland** died of an accidental overdose of barbiturates in the bathroom of her London flat.
- On January 3, 2008, **Natasha Collins**, an English actress and model, died in her bathtub after ingesting five times the lethal amount of cocaine. Alcohol was also involved. Her fiancé, children's television host Mark Speight, hanged himself four months later.

•

There is apparently no truth to the oft-told tale that a woman aboard an SAS aircraft was sealed to the toilet for the duration of the flight. However, on September 22, 1986, a seventy-year-old passenger on the Greek ship *Pegasus*, moored in Vancouver—it was there to accommodate visitors to the city's Expo—had a length of intestine sucked from her person when she operated a

{ **A seventy-year-old passenger on the Greek ship *Pegasus* had a length of intestine sucked from her person when she operated a vacuum flush toilet.** }

vacuum flush toilet while astride the convenience. The incident was reported in a cautionary letter written by Dr. J. Brendan Wynne, who said that "her buttocks and thighs completely occluded the opening of the toilet seat, causing the full force of the vacuum to be applied to the (pelvic) area." She was treated in Royal Columbian Hospital—a ten-day stay—and released, apparently tucked up and intact.

•

On February 27, 2008, police in Ness City, Kansas, were called to the home of Kory McFarren, where they pried the seat off the toilet upon which his girlfriend, **Pam Babcock**, had perched for two years. Her flesh and the plastic ring had, over that time, become as one. Mr. McFarren told police that he had, over the course of Miss Babcock's voluntary confinement, provided her with food and water and requested, with some regularity, that she rejoin the world. Always her reply would be, "Maybe tomorrow." Tomorrow, apparently, never came for poor Pam Babcock, whose story is as macabre as it is sad and whose outcome, at the time of this writing, remains uncertain.

J

Dear Old Father William,

I haven't heard back from you about the inquiry from my publisher friend, so I am going to take silence as acquiescence. I'm showing her the lists. Who knows, perhaps she'll want to do something with them? I'd like to be part of a book's birth, rather than its death, for once.

Apropos, while wasting time this morning grazing the fields of eBay, I happened to note a book for sale, a signed first-edition copy of Elizabeth Taylor's 1965 autobiography. If only I had a spare $650 rattling about in my handbag, I'd nab it and donate it to someone who could use it: yourself, for instance. Described as a "near fine copy with a trace of edgewear in a near fine dust jacket," its inscription reads: "To Darrell, Best wishes, Elizabeth Taylor." What on earth Darrell

J

was thinking when he let this treasure slip through his fingers is mostly what I wonder; not that I suppose I'll ever know.

In lieu of Elizabeth Taylor, I'm sending along this copy—battered but still serviceable—of Percy Dearmer's Parson's Handbook. If you've been wondering about the proper way to wear a tippet or an alb, or how best to fold and store altar cloths, this is for you.

J.N.

Instructions for better living

How to Visit the Ill (Advice to Parsons)

Avoid visiting dangerous cases of illness with an empty stomach, or with lungs exhausted by a quick ascent of the stairs. It may be well to take a biscuit and a glass of wine before going out; but above all things the priest should go in a spirit of calmness and faith. . . .

The cassock is an ideal protective garment from the medical point of view, but it should be of silk or other close material. Immediately on leaving the patient it should be taken off, given a good shake, and hung in the air for six hours; and the parson should air his clothes by a short walk. Indeed, he should never enter his own, or any other house, until he has thus aired his person.

In cases of virulent infection (such as small-pox, typhus, or scarlet fever in the peeling stage) the cassock as well as the surplice should be stoved; and if a stole is used, it should be treated in the same manner. It is best to dispense with a burse altogether and to boil the corporals and purificator.

The vestments should be of linen, for preference white or blue, and always washed after use.

The priest should never place himself between an infectious patient and the fire; for the air will then be drawn over his person.

He should not inhale the breath of the patient.

He should not keep his hand in contact with that of the patient.

After leaving the sick-room he should wash his hands at once. Soap and water, used thoroughly with a nail-brush, are enough in most cases, but soap and water with Jeye's fluid or carbolic acid are better. The hands should then be thoroughly rinsed with water. In severe cases he may use a solution of corrosive sublimate, having first removed any gold or silver rings. Soloids of the sublimate, manufactured by Burroughs and Welcome, can be got at any chemist's; one soloid is to be dissolved in a pint of water. If the patient has coughed any matter on to the priest's face, he should also wash his face in the solution.

He should never eat any food in an infectious house.

When he is much among infectious cases, as during an epidemic, he should take a hot bath every night, and a Turkish bath once a week.

—Percy Dearmer, *The Parson's Handbook* (6th edition, 1907)

The Driving and the Driven

Old Father William is just a tad embarrassed to admit that he already owns a copy of the Elizabeth Taylor memoir mentioned by Jane Nurse. I was deeply affected, when I was a boy, by her work in *National Velvet* and *Ivanhoe*, and ever since have been possessed of a sort of photographic memory for all things Taylorian. One of the anecdotes Miss Taylor offers in her book, from the vast store available to her, concerns a kerfuffle on the set of *Cleopatra*. Rex Harrison, cast as Caesar, was offended when his limousine was replaced with a more modest town car, and when he learned that his chauffeur was paid less than Miss Taylor's chauffeur. Always an advocate of pay equity, Mr. Harrison asked, "Why the hell should Elizabeth Taylor's chauffeur get more than my chauffeur just because she has a bigger chest?"

Here are some other chauffeur–client relationships that might have been improved through therapy or some other form of intervention.

Enrico Caruso

His driver in his later years was "the faithful Fitzgerald," who ferried him around in a little green Lancia. Caruso's earlier days were fraught, and the object of salacious public curiosity. In 1906, he was arrested for allegedly groping a woman in the monkey house of the Central Park Zoo. A few years later, he was the object of blackmail attempts by a Mafia-like ring, the Black Hand. And there was much tittering, in Italy and abroad, when the soprano Ada Giachetti, Caruso's long-time paramour and the mother of four of his children—only two of whom survived infancy—dumped him for their chauffeur, Cesare Romati; the press made much hay with how they eloped, and in the tenor's very own car, what's more. The conniving pair then tried to extort money from the famous tenor, for which, in 1912, they were tried and convicted. While leaving the courtroom in Milan, Romati made a "theatrical gesture" and shouted, "It's not all over with Caruso yet!"

Phyllis Diller

On May 28, 2001, Patricia Marcella, forty-four, was killed in the line of duty while she was driving comedienne Phyllis Diller to a hotel in, or nearby, Cambridge, Ontario. When Ms Marcella stopped to ask directions, she parked on an uphill incline and left the limo in neutral. As she was passing behind the car, it rolled and killed her. Miss Diller was unharmed, as was Mercer Helms, a magician, who was with her in the back seat. Miss Diller, at the time of this writing, is extant, exploring life in her nineties, and no longer performing. Mr. Helms, a barnacled veteran, is still at it and is sometimes billed—not too often, one hopes—as "former opening act for Phyllis Diller."

Various Roosevelts

On November 6, 1910, Alexander Ehbel, chauffeur to John Ellis Roosevelt, fifth cousin to ex-president Theodore Roosevelt, was killed after relinquishing the wheel to his employer while on a road trip. The car "turned turtle," breaking Mr. Ehbel's neck and crushing his skull. Mr. Roosevelt escaped with minor injuries.

Six years later, according to the *New York Times* (September 11, 1916), police were looking for John Stolburg, chauffeur to Theodore Roosevelt Jr. Mr. Stolburg had taken his employer's car without permission and smashed it up. Mr. Roosevelt seemed calm, perhaps remembering the advice of his famous father to speak softly and carry a big stick shift.

When the ex-president died a few years later, his bodyguard, Charlie Lee, became Mrs. Roosevelt's chauffeur. The son of a slave who was once indentured to Robert E. Lee, Charlie Lee made the news when Mrs. Roosevelt awarded him his pension at the age of sixty. That was in 1934; *Time* noted that Roosevelt's "original big stick" was hanging on the wall of Mr. Lee's home.

Yoko Ono

Shortly before Christmas 2006, Koral Karsan, Yoko Ono's chauffeur, tried to wrest two million dollars from his employer, saying that he had potentially embarrassing recordings that he would release to the press. The authorities were summoned. In January 2007, the *New York Times* reported Mr. Karsan's disclosure that his job was so stressful that he had lost eight teeth through nocturnal grinding. After serving sixty days in jail, he brokered a deal with the prosecution that allowed him to plead guilty to a lesser charge than extortion. He was released in time to attend his son's wedding, which must have been a relief to all concerned.

Marcel Proust

On May 30, 1914, near Antibes, France, Alfred Agostinelli, a novice pilot on his second solo flight, did an Icarus and fell from the sky and into the sea. He wasn't killed on impact, indeed, was standing up calling for help—not drowning, but waving—before being hauled under when his craft submerged. He was, for a time, Marcel Proust's chauffeur and the unwilling recipient of poor, asthmatic, logorrheic Marcel's attention.

Francis Rattenbury

George Percy Stoner was the young chauffeur to Francis and Alma Rattenbury. Francis was a celebrated Canadian architect, transplanted to the Villa Madeira, in Bournemouth, England, and Alma was his pretty, vivacious, much younger wife. Things became hot and heavy between George and Alma, and they decided to deal with the problem of Francis by applying a mallet to his skull. Well, George did the applying. His death sentence was commuted to life in prison. He served seven years and died at eighty-three, on March 24, 2000, the sixty-fifth anniversary of the murder. Alma was acquitted, but committed suicide soon afterwards by plunging a knife into her heart on the banks of the river Avon. Francis Rattenbury's grave was unmarked until 2007, when a family friend arranged for a headstone.

Dwight D. Eisenhower

Eisenhower's Irish chauffeur and confidante during the Second World War, Kay Summersby, published two accounts of their time together. The chummy *Ike Was My Boss* came out in 1947, and the somewhat steamier *Past Forgetting: My Love Affair with Dwight D. Eisenhower* was published posthumously in 1975. The Tab A/Slot B business—which is what we're mostly interested in, let's face it—seemed never to amount to anything. The driving, it appears, never achieved the metaphorical.

Pierre Pettigrew

Bruno Labonté was the chauffeur and security adviser to a Canadian minister of foreign affairs, Pierre Pettigrew. For a tedious time, round about 2005, M. Labonté's name was bandied about and somewhat sullied by the sniping Canadian press, whose diabolical agents speculated unkindly and with much nudge-nudge-wink-winkery about the nature of the relationship between the minister and his driver, who accompanied his boss on any number of foreign excursions where there was, apparently, no need of a driver and not so very much of a security requirement either. Unscrupulous hacks even published a leaked memo from the minister's office, from 2004, which said, "Please be advised that Bruno Labonté, Minister's driver and security, is to have a Blanket Travel Authorisation when traveling with the Minister at all times." Old Father William wonders just what might be the problem with a chauffeur wanting a blanket; also, he feels that if there's even a remote chance that jumper cables might need to be applied, whether by day or by night, it's best to have a professional along to work the clamps.

The Mayor of Worcester

Another English story. Mr. Stan Brookes was the chauffeur to Margaret Layland, the Mayor of Worcester, when it was revealed that Mr. Brookes was providing lap dancing services, both in the official car and on the sofa of the mayoral parlour. Much embarrassment ensued, but Mr. Brookes saved face somewhat when he told the *Sunday Mirror,* "We never had sex when we should have been working. And I never claimed hours for work when we had been making love."

Benito Mussolini

Signor Ercole Boratto, once an Alfa Romeo test driver, was Mussolini's chauffeur from 1922 to 1943. Immediately after the war, Boratto wrote a memoir at the behest of some occupying official, in exchange for a small truck and on the condition that it not be published in his lifetime. He died in 1970 and the memoir languished, forgotten, until it was discovered quite by accident by a researcher who had something else in mind. It's a colourful description of life with Il Duce, whose rapacious sexual appetites have long been well known. On February 29, 2008, the highly customized Alfa Romeo 6C 2300 Pescara Spyder in which Mussolini had been squired around and with which Boratto won the Mille Miglia road race in 1936 failed to reach its reserve bid when it was put up for auction in Cheltenham.

J

Dear Old Father William,

I would never have pegged you as the type to be interested in the celebrity biography; they are a guilty pleasure of mine, too. To perhaps provide you with another perspective on the making of Cleopatra—surely one of the most garish films of all time—I have removed from the library, perhaps just a little ahead of its time, this copy of The Incomparable Rex, by Patrick Garland. He always gave me the creeps, Rex I mean, although I confess that as a much younger woman I had a kind of crush on his son, the folksinger, sort of, Noel Harrison. I think his version of "The Windmills of Your Mind" was definitive. That I actually hold an opinion about such a thing makes me just a little concerned.

J.N.

How to Make a Cabbage Centrepiece

Take a head of cabbage, one that has been picked too late is best, for the leaves open better then, and are apt to be slightly curled. Lay the cabbage on a flat plate or salver and press the leaves down and open with your hand, firmly but gently, so as not to break them off. When they all lie out flat, stab the firm, yellow heart through several times with a sharp knife, until its outlines are lost, and then place flowers at random all over the cabbage.

Roses are prettiest, but any flower which has a firm, stiff stem, capable of holding the blossom upright, will do. Press the stems down through the leaves and put in sufficient green to vary prettily. The outer leaves of the cabbage, the only ones to be seen when the flowers are in, form a charming background, far prettier than any basket. Roses are best for all seasons, but autumn offers some charming variations. The brilliant scarlet berries of the mountain ash or red thorn mingled with the deep, rich green of feathery asparagus, make a delicious color symphony most appropriate to the season.

—*Vaughan's Vegetable Cook Book* (4th edition, 1919)

Good and Faithful Servants

Every valet shall be exalted. Isn't that what the Bible tells us? Rex Harrison's long-time valet—as I read in Jane Nurse's latest gift book—was Walter Massey. Massey's predecessor was a fellow named Tosh whose last assignment for Harrison was transporting some Herbert Johnson hats from Los Angeles to New York. When Harrison learned that Tosh had been murdered in California he said, allegedly, "And now I suppose I'll never get my hats."

Here's a way to test your knowledge of servants and masters. In Column 1 is an alphabetical list of some factotums, amanuenses, and others of the helping ilk. Match them with their employers, also listed alphabetically, in Column 2. Answers and brief bios follow.

Servants	Masters
Barnett, Marilyn	Brando, Marlon
Beckett, Samuel	Caruso, Enrico
Bethell, Agnes Jean	Chaplin, Charlie
Brown, Rosemary	Cohan, George M.
Cabreira, Vera Lúcia	Crawford, Joan
Centra, Pio	Frost, Robert
Doda, Bayazid Elmas	Gardner, Erle Stanley
Dugdale, Florence	Hardy, Thomas
Gandy, Helen	Hoover, J. Edgar
Hirano, Michio (Mike)	Joyce, James
Kono, Toraichi	King, Billie Jean
Marchak, Alice	Leo XIII, Pope
Morrison, Kathleen	Liszt, Franz
Smith, Jeri Binder	Niemeyer, Oscar
Wood, Ursula	Nopcsa, Baron Franz
Zirato, Bruno	Vaughan Williams, Ralph

Marilyn Barnett

Secretary and ball-girl for tennis ace **Billie Jean King**, Ms. Barnett brought a palimony suit against Ms King in 1981.

Samuel Beckett

For a time, during the long composition of *Finnegan's Wake,* amanuensis to **James Joyce**.

Agnes Jean Bethell

The model for Perry Mason's secretary, Della Street, was the long-time secretary to Mason's creator, **Erle Stanley Gardner**. Her sisters, Honey and Peggy, were also thus engaged. Gardner cranked out seven thousand words a day and employed up to seven secretaries at a time to keep up with the volume: a secretary pool with a very deep end, evidently. Mr. Gardner married Agnes Jean in 1968. She died in 2002, at the age of one hundred.

Rosemary Brown

An English housewife, Mrs. Brown was the amanuensis to composers who had crossed over, and claimed to receive musical dictation from, among others, **Liszt**, Chopin, and Debussy. She was essentially untrained, but her received compositions bear strong stylistic traces of their putative otherside creators.

Vera Lúcia Cabreira

Secretary to **Oscar Niemeyer**, Brazilian architect and design mastermind of Brasília. On November 10, 2006, Ms. Cabreira, aged sixty, became Mrs. Niemeyer when she married her boss, who was a few days shy of ninety-nine.

Pio Centra

Centra was the valet to **Pope Leo XIII**, who died at the age of ninety-three, which means he holds the record as oldest pope. He lingered over his withering, and the press of the day was fond of reporting how Centra was ever at his side, refusing to rest. When the Pope finally released his soul into the keeping of whatever comes next, on July 20, 1903, Centra said that he wouldn't be long in following. He lasted until December 17, 1904.

Bayazid Elmas Doda

Secretary, lover, and companion-in-fossils to the paleontologist and aspirant to the Albanian throne **Baron Franz Nopcsa**. Their lives ended in 1933 when the baron shot Mr. Doda and then himself. As his secretary was not available to take dictation, Baron Nopcsa wrote his own farewell note: "The motive for my suicide is a nervous breakdown. The reason that I shot my longtime friend and secretary, Mr. Bayazid Elmas Doda, in his sleep without his suspecting at all is that I did not wish to leave him behind sick, in misery and without a penny, because he would have suffered too much. I wish to be cremated."

Florence Dugdale

Married her boss, **Thomas Hardy**, in 1914. She had been his secretary since 1905 and was forty years younger than he. Her first career had been as a writer of children's books.

Helen Gandy

Unusually, seems not to have indulged in carnal relations with her boss, who was FBI director **J. Edgar Hoover.** In his employ for fifty-four years, Miss Gandy oversaw the shredding of many juicy files after Mr. Hoover's death in 1972.

Michio "Mike" Hirano

For many years the valet of composer **George M. Cohan**, at least according to Scott Sandage. In an article in *Cabinet Magazine* (Summer 2002) he describes how Hirano, through occasional stage and radio appearances, became a minor celebrity himself, and how Cohan, the ailing but still living embodiment of Yankee Doodle Dandyism, tried to intervene on his behalf post-Pearl Harbor, but to no avail. Hirano vanished.

Toraichi Kono

Kono was born in Hiroshima in 1888 and came to the United States as a young man. In 1916, he answered an ad from an unnamed potential employer who was on the lookout for a chauffeur. The boss-in-waiting proved to be **Charlie Chaplin**, and Kono became his secretary/valet. That relationship lasted until 1934, at which point there was a rift between the two involving Chaplin's third wife, Paulette Goddard. Kono remained in the United Artists orbit for a few years until accusations of espionage and the Second World War saw to his rerouting. He eventually returned to Hiroshima and died there in 1971.

Alice Marchak

Secretary to **Marlon Brando** and, for a time, the legal guardian of Mr. Brando's troubled son, Christian, who died in January 2008. Miss Marchak is the co-author of a book called *The Super Secs: Behind the Scenes with the Secretaries of the Superstars.*

Kathleen Morrison

Mrs. Morrison was secretary to **Robert Frost** from 1938 until the poet's death in 1963. The relationship had its ambiguities. She was married to Theodore Morrison, who taught creative writing at Harvard.

Jeri Binder Smith

Joan Crawford's secretary for a time in the fifties. In 1998, she told the *New York Daily News* that Crawford would "soak in the tub and have me sit on the toilet to take dictation." Smith's duties also included calling Crawford's fans to let them know where the star would be dining, so that an entourage would be in place when she arrived.

Ursula Wood

A poet and librettist, she was secretary to the composer **Ralph Vaughan Williams** and married him, in a decorous way, after the death of his wife. She was forty-one; he was eighty. She was president of the English Folk Dance and Song Society and died in 2007, aged ninety-six.

Bruno Zirato

In *The Life and Death of Caruso,* Dorothy **Caruso** writes of her husband's factotum,

> Zirato wasn't a trained secretary. No professional could have held the position for a day, for although he was highly paid, he had no time to himself, no regular hours; he had to do anything Enrico asked, and at any time, regardless of his personal feelings. His inexpertness at the typewriter was more than balanced by the speed with which he used two fingers, and his prodigious memory aided the unique method he had invented to keep in order letters, accounts, lists, clippings, albums, collections, engagements, messages, and people.

Dear Jane Nurse,

Thanks for the copy "signed by the author, no less!" of John O'Brien's Winning Converts: Catholic evangelism has never been one of my enduring fascinations, but it's never too late. Which is, I guess, one of the messages of the book. I'm particularly taken with the photographs, especially the one of the fun-loving group captioned, "These are the trailer catechists, eleven of whom are converts. One became a Sister of Mercy at Nashville, Tenn."

I am inclined to think, Jane Nurse, that you are sending me a not-so-subtle message. I don't require conversion, especially, to your publishing idea. It's all the same to me, really. I just don't want you to go to any trouble. All that typing!

O.F.W.

Dear O.F.W.,

In my life I have won but one trophy, and that was in a high school typing contest. I'm embarrassed to report that I have it still.

J.N.

A Ribbon of Facts about
a Few Types of Typists

Theodora Bosanquet was secretary to **Henry James** from 1907 until his death in 1916. She took down his ornate sentences on a Remington typewriter. Henry James especially appreciated the sound of the Remington, which was the brand of machine **Adolf Hitler** used to write *Mein Kampf* and that **Ray Bradbury** rented in 1950, for ten cents on the half-hour in the Powell Library at UCLA, to write the first draft of his novel about book burning, *Fahrenheit 451*.

•

The hugely prolific **Enid Blyton** would, on a good day, write between six and ten thousand words. She explained how:

> I shut my eyes for a few minutes, with my portable typewriter on my knees—I make my mind go blank and wait—and then, as clearly as I would see real children, my characters stand before me in my mind's eye. . . . As I look at them, the characters take on movement and life— they talk and laugh, and I hear them. . . . The story is enacted in my mind's eye almost as if I had a private cinema screen there. . . . I watch and hear everything, writing it down with my typewriter.

Who could have suspected the author of the Noddy books and *The Secret Seven* of having so mystical, hermetic a method of composition?

•

Stanley Kunitz, the American poet, was a lifelong user of the Hermes typewriter. **William Gibson** wrote *Neuromancer* on a Hermes 2000. **Larry McMurtry** made a point of thanking his Hermes 3000 typewriter at the Golden Globes in 2006, in accepting the award for the screenplay for *Brokeback Mountain*. The screenplay also won an Academy Award, as, in 2008, did the adaptation of **Cormac McCarthy**'s *No Country for Old Men*. McCarthy works on an Olivetti manual.

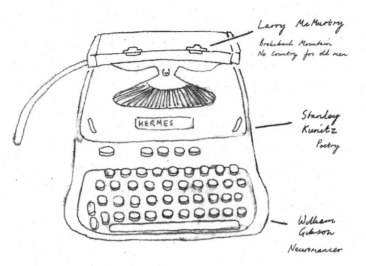

Screenwriter **Helen Deutsch,** who won a Golden Globe for the 1953 Leslie Caron vehicle *Lili,* and was also responsible for *The Unsinkable Molly Brown, National Velvet,* and *King Solomon's Mines,* never learned to type. She relied on a Dictaphone. Her last screen project, in 1967, was the memorable adaptation of *Valley of the Dolls.* **Jacqueline Susann** wrote the original property on an Olympia typewriter.

Jacqueline Susann's arch-nemesis at the time of writing *Valley of the Dolls* was **Truman Capote,** who was a childhood friend of **Harper Lee**; he turns up as Dill in *To Kill a Mockingbird.* It was during one of their summers together, in Alabama, that Lee's father brought home her first typewriter, a battle-scarred Underwood. Capote liked to work in longhand, to begin, using a Number 2 pencil. In 1957, he told the *Paris Review,* "I am a completely horizontal author. I can't think unless I am lying down, either in bed or stretched on a couch, and with a cigarette and coffee handy."

Mark Twain, who was also fond of writing in bed, was one of the first writers to submit a typewritten manuscript, in 1874. He wrote *Life on the Mississippi* at the rate of nineteen words per minute on a Sholes & Glidden machine, having brought himself up to speed by consecrating to the page, over and over again, the line, "The boy stood on the burning deck." Sholes & Glidden typewriters were made by Remington.

•

Darren Wershler-Henry, in his book *The Iron Whim,* describes how **Northrop Frye**, the Canadian literary critic, came from Moncton to Toronto in 1929 to compete in an Underwood typing contest and came in second in the novice class, with a speed of sixty-three words per minute. He soon increased his speed to eighty-five words per minute.

•

Jack Kerouac could crank it out at the rate of a hundred words per minute on an Underwood, which brings to mind Truman Capote's famous assessment of *On the Road:* "That's not writing, it's typing." Kerouac typed *Naked Lunch* for **William S. Burroughs**, himself the scion of the Burroughs family, maker of adding machines and typewriters.

•

Kerouac did his amanuensis routine in the Chelsea Hotel, an institution immortalized by **Leonard Cohen**, who wrote his song "Suzanne" on an olive-green Olivetti 22 portable that he bought in London in 1959 for forty pounds. **Herb Caen**, the celebrated columnist for the *San Francisco Chronicle,* was a fast two-finger typist and pounded out fifty-seven years' worth of columns on a Royal. **Dashiell Hammett**'s Royal is, or has been, on display in the San Francisco Public Library. **Ernest Hemingway** was likewise a Royal user; one account has him thumping away with the machine balanced on top of a copy of *Who's Who in America.* Hemingway wasn't loyal to the Royal; he also used the Corona No. 3 and No. 4, the Underwood Noiseless Portable, and a Halda portable.

Tintinnabulation

The ping of the typewriter bell, that sweet warning of the imminent necessity of the carriage's return, is one of the sounds that is mostly lost to us in this marvellous and awful century. Now it's mostly heard only in pop concerts when someone thinks to program "The Typewriter," by Leroy Anderson. Bells, generally speaking, are not nearly so much a part of the public soundscape as was once the case. In most North American cities, it's rare to hear them ringing out to mark the passing of the hours or to summon the faithful to worship. And it's not just the pealing that's lost to us; ritual, too, suffers a kind of decay. Old Father William, with cultural preservation and his readers' best interests at heart, offers these several instructional cullings from the quite vast body of bell literature (not quite *belles lettres,* but close enough for family, as it were).

•

In her landmark book on etiquette, published in 1922 and endlessly revised, Emily Post gives these directions for the draping of the doorbell after a death in the family:

> As a rule the funeral director hangs crepe streamers on the bell; white ones for a child, black and white for a young person, or black for an older person. This signifies to the passerby that it is a house of mourning so that the bell will not be rung unnecessarily nor long.
>
> If they prefer, the family sometimes orders a florist to hang a bunch of violets or other purple flowers on black ribbon streamers, for a grown person; or white violets, white carnations—any white flower without leaves—on the black ribbon for a young woman or man; or white flowers on white gauze or ribbon for a child.

•

John Brocas was buried on February 22, 1662, after getting caught up, quite literally, in his work, and accidentally hanging himself on his bell rope in the church of Axminster.

•

In *The Parson's Handbook*, Reverend Percy Dearmer has this advice on how to ring bells for the dead and the dying:

> The passing bell should always be rung before death; the reason of this ancient custom being that the faithful may pray for the dying person. Canon 67 orders: "When any is passing out of this life, a bell shall be tolled, and the Minister shall not then slack to do his last duty. And after the party's death, if it so fall out, there shall be rung no more than one short peal, and one other before the burial, and one other after the burial."
>
> It is customary to toll a minute bell also before the funeral, quickening the time when the procession is in sight and stopping when it reaches the lych-gate. A handbell may well be rung before the funeral procession, in accordance with ancient custom, from the moment it leaves the house.
>
> The old usage at the time of death, known as the Passing Bell, was to toll a certain number of strokes, with "Tellers" at the beginning and end, usually three times three for a male, three times two for a woman. Sometimes parishes use three single strokes in the case of a child, others distinguish children or infants by the use of one of the smaller bells in place of the tenor which is ordinarily used.

•

Livelier instructions for the use of bells can be found in Cecil J. Sharp's *The Morris Book* (1907), a didactic tome intended for the use of Morris dancers:

> The Morris-men wear bells strapped to their shins; the bells are there that they may ring their music—and a fine wholesome music it is, too: to ring, they must be well shaken; to be shaken, the leg they are strapped

to must be kicked and stamped. Get that principle into your head, and that practice into your legs, and you make the first long stride towards acquisition of the art of Morris dancing. Strap a set of bells to your shins, get out upon a grass-plot or the King's highway; never mind elegance or the criticism of the emasculate modern: kick and stamp upon the earth in such a manner as to make your bells ring their loudest, and ring all together. You will see pretty soon that, to [make your bells ring their loudest], you must, when you jump, let the heels come solidly to earth, immediately following the toes—no man, even an old-time Morris-man, may jump and alight upon his heels alone, with the spine held rigidly above them. You will find also that, in stepping it, whether to advance or retire, or to step rhythmically in one place, to make your bells ring the true fortissimo you must kick, and kick hard.

•

Cecil Sharp, a principal in the folk revival in Great Britain in the early years of the century, would be pleased to see the perpetuation of these instructions for the proper christening of church bells. The source is Tanswell's *History of Lambeth* (1858):

1, The bell must be first baptized before it may be hung in the steeple; 2, the bell must be baptized by a bishop or his deputy; 3, in the baptism of the bell there is used holy water, oil, salt, cream &c.; 4, the bell must have godfathers, and they must be persons of high rank; 5, the bell must be washed by the hand of a bishop; 6, the bell must be solemnly crossed by the bishop; 7, the bell must be anointed by the bishop; 8, the bell must be washed and anointed in the name of the Trinity; 9, at the baptism of the bell they pray literally for the bell. The following is part of the curious prayers used at the above ceremony:

"Lord, grant that whatsoever this holy bell, thus washed and baptized and blessed, shall sound, all deceits of Satan, and danger of whirlwind, thunder and lightning, and tempests, may be driven away, and that devotion may increase in Christian men when they hear it. . . . And grant, Lord, that all that come to the church at the sound of it may be free from all temptations of the devil."

•

In Venice, it was likewise the custom to name and anoint bells. Nevertheless, the campanile in the Piazza San Marco, which had stood firm since its completion on July 6, 1515, crumbled on July 14, 1902. Four of the five bells were destroyed. They were recast and installed in the new campanile and were ready for ringing in 1912.

The old names for the five bells were the *Marangona,* by whose ringing the various craftsmen of the various guilds knew when to begin and to stop work and which also advised the city councillors that meetings were about to begin; the *Trottiera,* which was used in conjunction with the *Marangona* to let said councillors know that their horses were going to have to trot if they wanted to get there in time; the *Nona,* which rang out at midday; the *Mezza Terra,* which announced the meetings of the Senate; and the *Renghiera* or *Maleficio,* which was the smallest of the five, and was rung to announce the imminence of an execution. In *Venice and Its Lagoon,* the *sine qua non* guidebook to the city, Giulio Lorenzetti writes,

> The Campanile is associated with various circumstances: the well-known supplizio della cheba (the torture cage) when the victim was shut up in an iron cage hung by a cord on the south face of the tower, night and day; the traditional festival of the svolo dell'Angelo (flight of the Angel) or del Turco, which was a sort of acrobatic display consisting of a skillfully accomplished slide down a tight rope from the height of the Belfry as far as a boat in the Pool of San Marco and then to the Ducal Palace where the Doge and the Signoria were watching. This took place every Thursday before Lent.

•

Lorenzetti promises thirty-six "easy ramps" between the entrance to the campanile and the viewing platform at the top. Here are some other locations and statistics that will be of interest to altitude aspirants who suffer from clautophobia, as the fear of elevators is named, or who, for their own good reasons, would simply prefer to climb the stairs:

Location	Steps
Spanish Steps, Rome	138
Potemkin Stairs, Odessa	192
John Hancock Tower, Boston	1,062
Bell Atlantic Tower, Philadelphia	1,088
Emirates Towers, Dubai	1,136
Bank of America Center, San Francisco	1,197
Azrieli Tower, Tel Aviv	1,300
Swissôtel, Singapore	1,336
US Bank Tower, Los Angeles	1,500
Sky Tower, Auckland	1,504
Sydney Tower, Sydney	1,504
Empire State Building, New York	1,576
John Hancock Center, Chicago	1,632
Eiffel Tower, Paris	1,665
Jin Mao Tower, Shanghai	2,008
Taipei 101, Taipei	2,046
KL Tower, Kuala Lumpur	2,058
Sears Tower, Chicago	2,109
CN Tower, Toronto	2,579
Niesen Stairway	11,674

(the longest stairway in the world, following the path of the funicular up Mt. Niesen, Switzerland)

"You are old," said the youth, "one would hardly suppose
That your eye was as steady as ever;
Yet you balanced an eel on the end of your nose—
What made you so awfully clever?"

"I have answered three questions, and that is enough,"
Said his father. "Don't give yourself airs!
Do you think I can listen all day to such stuff?
Be off, or I'll kick you down-stairs!"

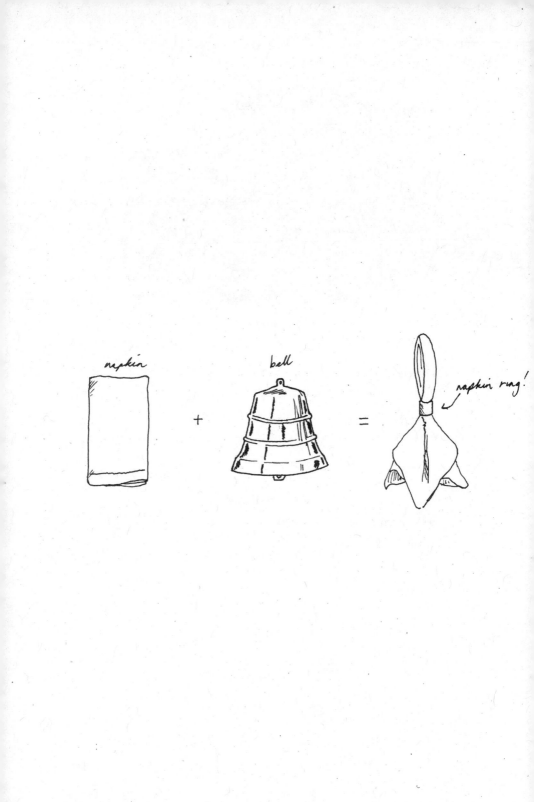

napkin + bell = napkin ring!

⸺ How to Use Napkins ⸺

Napkin rings are unknown in fashionable houses outside of the nursery. But in large families where it is impossible to manage such a wash as three clean napkins a day entail, napkin rings are probably necessary. In most moderately run houses, a napkin that is unrumpled and spotless after a meal is put aside and used again for breakfast; but to be given a napkin that is not perfectly clean is a horrid thought. Perhaps though, the necessity for napkin rings results in the achievement of the immaculate napkin—which is quite a nice thought.

—Emily Post, *Etiquette in Society, in Business, in Politics and at Home* (1922)

Warhol's Butterflies
and Other Enduring Ephemera

J ane Nurse has been oddly quiet about the business of ushering my jottings into print; not that I'm concerned, mind you. Not that I devote any of my precious time to wondering whether or not I'll join the overcrowded ranks of the published. Not that I particularly care if these random musings pitch their tent on the campground of posterity. If I did care—and have I mentioned that I do not?—then I could take some solace in knowing that even the most seemingly disposable of doodles will stand the test of time.

·

The Scottish architect **Sir Basil Spence**, on a visit to Wellington in 1964, had dinner with New Zealand's prime minister. Perhaps during a lull in the conversation, he took a napkin and sketched the preliminary design for the "Beehive," which is now the executive wing of the New Zealand Parliament. The building was completed in 1981. Recent renovations included the construction of a bombproof mailroom—it saddens Old Father William to think that we have made a world where such innovations are required.

·

David Bellamy, one of the two Bellamy Brothers of country music fame, wrote the duo's 1979 hit, "If I Said You Had a Beautiful Body Would You Hold It against Me," on the back of a napkin.

·

One night in 1983, **Andy Warhol** (see also *When Wigs Go Wrong*), having dinner at Diana Vreeland's, drew butterflies on some dinner linen. The napkin, through a series of complicated circumstances, made its way to Honolulu and into the hands of a man named Kevin, who, in the fullness of time, made inquiries about its worth to the *Antiques Roadshow*. He was referred to the Warhol Foundation, the final arbiter when it comes to questions of

Warholian authenticity. The tests came back positive: the butterflies were indeed Andy's; also, apparently, the food stains.

•

The Seattle Space Needle began its life as a doodle on the back of a cocktail napkin, in Stuttgart, in 1959. The doodler was airline and hotel executive **Edward E. Carlson**.

•

Stuttgart is a scant seventy-nine kilometres from Heidelberg, where **Erica Jong** lived in the mid-sixties with her second husband, Alan Jong. In her essay "A Twenty-first Century Ritual," she says that she married her fourth husband, Ken Burrows, a divorce lawyer, only once they were both signatories to a contract, drafted on a napkin, that stipulated he wouldn't interfere with her writing. Ten years later, they found and burned the item, deciding it was no longer necessary. Its validity might have been in question, to judge from **Amy Irving**'s successful contestation of her back-of-a-napkin prenuptial agreement with **Steven Spielberg**. Apparently, no legal advice was available tableside; she received a settlement of around a hundred million dollars.

AMY IRVING'S
LAWYER'S NAPKIN

$100.000.000.000.00

•

In 1950, while attending a peace conference in Sheffield, **Pablo Picasso** drew a dove on a napkin in Butler's Dining Rooms. Later, in London, he duplicated the feat and gave the drawing as a gift to his security guard.

•

Bartolomé Esteban Murillo (1617–82) was commissioned to execute some paintings for the Franciscan Convento de los Capuchinos, in Seville. One of these, a Virgin and Child, apparently a tribute to the cook of this Capuchin brotherhood (the fryer to the friars, one supposes) was done on a napkin. *La Virgen de la Servilleta,* as it is popularly known, now hangs in the Museo de Bellas Artes in Seville. Murillo is memorialized on the northern shores of Lake Superior by the tiny town of Murillo, where the annual fall fair features chariot races.

•

Fairs the world over feature Ferris wheels, named for **George Washington Gale Ferris Jr.**, who answered a call for an American challenge to the splendours of the Eiffel Tower, something to show off Yankee ingenuity at the Chicago World's Fair. He scribbled down the first design on a napkin at an engineer's dinner in 1891, and the inaugural spin took place on June 15, 1893. Ferris died in 1896, a beaten man, after his efforts to capitalize on his success with the wheel came to naught. His wife, toasted on that glorious June day, left him a few months before he did the mortal coil shuffle. He was cremated, and his ashes remained unclaimed for fifteen months after incineration: a sad end when so self-evident a scenario for scattering suggested itself.

•

The Laffer Curve, an economic touchstone that charts—at least, to people who can read it—the relationship between tax rates and tax revenue, was sketched in 1974 by economist **Arthur Laffer** on the back of a napkin when he was having lunch with, among others, Dick Cheney.

•

"To take action to bring women into full participation in the mainstream of American society now, exercising all privileges and responsibilities thereof in truly equal partnership with men." This statement of purpose, written on a napkin by **Betty Friedan** in 1966, became the founding document of the National Organization for Women.

•

In a universe-balancing gesture, the scorned-by-feminists screenwriter **Joe Eszterhas**, author of such putatively misogynistic screenplays as *Basic Instinct* and *Showgirls,* allegedly received an advance of four million dollars for the napkin-scribbled outline of what eventually evolved into the film *One Night Stand.* It bombed.

•

Speaking of bombs, **Philip Morrison**, **Sydney Dancoff**, and **Joseph Weinberg**, all students attached to the laboratory of J. Robert Oppenheimer, sketched an early prototype of an atomic device in a student union cafeteria, on a napkin.

•

In 1973, computer engineer **Robert Metcalfe** sketched out the basic precepts of Ethernet technologies on a napkin. It has been preserved in Palo Alto, in the archives of the Xerox Research Center.

A Litter of Literals

In 1996 Mr. Metcalfe, honouring a commitment he had made to "eat his words" if his prediction about an Internet crash proved incorrect, publicly pulped and downed, as a smoothie, the offending column. The writer and artist Douglas Coupland is another word eater: he created wasp's nests from pages of his own books, which he chewed while watching television.

Literally killed by kindness was Draco, who established the legal code of Athens and whose name lives on in the word "Draconian." According to the tenth-century encyclopedia the *Suda,* he'd crossed over to the island of Aegina "for lawgiving purposes and was being honoured by the Aeginetans in the theatre, but they threw so many hats and shirts and cloaks on his head that he suffocated, and was buried in that selfsame theatre."

And history records more than a few instances of those who, literally, died laughing. In the *Reader's Handbook* (1911), E. Cobham Brewer reports the following under the heading "Laughter, Death From":

> Crassus died from laughter on seeing an ass eat thistles. Margutte the giant died of laughter on seeing an ape trying to put on his boots. Philemon or Philomenes died of laughter on seeing an ass eat the figs provided for his own dinner. Zeuxis died of laughter at sight of a hag which he had just depicted. On April 19, 1782, Mrs. Fitzherbert died from laugher at the way C. Banister portrayed "Polly" in Gay's *Beggar's Opera* (1727) at Drury Lane Theatre.

In more recent years, the laughing, though not laughable, deaths of Ole Bentzen and Alex Mitchell have been amply reported. Mr. Bentzen, a Dane, was asphyxiated by hilarity while watching the John Cleese/Jamie Lee Curtis vehicle *A Fish Called Wanda.* Bentzen was an audiologist. An interesting homonym—audi to Oddie—links his demise to that of Mr. Mitchell. Bill Oddie was a member of the English comedy troupe The Goodies, who owed a certain amount to John Cleese and the Monty Python crew. An English bricklayer, Mr.

Mitchell was so tickled by an episode of *The Goodies* called "Kung Fu Kapers" that he laughed for the better part of half an hour and then keeled over; it was more than his heart could bear. He died in 1975 at the age of fifty.

Died at Fifty

- **Joe Strummer** (1952–2002), front man for the Clash.

- **Kurt Weill** (1900–50), composer of many theatrical works, most notably *Threepenny Opera* (based on *The Beggar's Opera*).

- **Herb Ritts** (1952–2002), fashion photographer.

- **Dave "Chico" Ryan** (1948–98), bassist and singer with Sha Na Na.

- **Raymond Carver** (1938–1988), American short story writer and poet.

- **Rod Serling** (1924–75), American screenwriter, driving force behind the TV series *The Twilight Zone;* Serling was born on Christmas Day.

- **Alban Berg** (1885–1935), hugely influential twentieth-century composer among whose works are the operas *Lulu* and *Wozzek.* Berg died, of an infection contracted from an insect bite, on Christmas Eve.

- **Marcello Viotti** (1954–2005), Swiss conductor, especially celebrated for his operatic turns. He was the director of La Fenice in Venice at the time of his death, of a stroke.

- **Alan Ladd** (1913–64), diminutive actor and frequent co-star of Veronica Lake. His last appearance was in the film adaptation of the Harold Robbins novel *The Carpetbaggers* (see *Polly Math*).

- **Max Baer** (1909–59), heavyweight boxing champion, actor, father of actor Max Baer Jr. (see also *Shaves Too Close for Comfort, Died in a Hotel*).

- **Carson McCullers** (1917–67), American writer, author of *The Heart Is a Lonely Hunter* and *The Ballad of the Sad Café*.

- **Glenn Hughes** (1952–2002), the leatherman clone in the Village People.

- **Gianni Versace** (1946–97), fashion mogul, founder of the house of Versace.

- **Gaetano Donizetti** (1797–1848), Italian composer of many, many bel canto operas (see also *Shedding Season*).

- **Lance Loud** (1951–2001), journalist and musician, founder of the band the Mumps, who came to prominence in *An American Family*, an early foray into the blight known as reality television.

- **Cozy Powell** (1947–98), English rock drummer, most notably with Black Sabbath, killed in a car crash while talking on his mobile phone.

- **Steve McQueen** (1930–80), American actor and motorcycle enthusiast.

- **Errol Flynn** (1909–59), swashbuckling actor, playboy, and genial miscreant. He died in Vancouver, in the Burnaby Street apartment of Dr.

The June 2002 edition of the magazine *Mortuary Management* notes that the friends of an English man who died on his fiftieth birthday went ahead and held his surprise party anyway.

Grant Gould. Dr. Gould was the uncle of **Glenn Gould** (1932–82). Glenn Gould, when he died at fifty, was particularly famous for his eccentricities and for his performances of music by J.S. Bach. Bach died at the age of sixty-five, but his father, **Johann Ambrosius Bach**, died on his fiftieth birthday (February 24, 1645–February 24, 1695). The composer **Praetorius** also died on his fiftieth birthday, on February 15, 1621—you do the math if you want to know his birth date—as did **Karl Eugen Neumann**, a translator of Buddhist texts, on October 18, 1915, ditto the calculation.

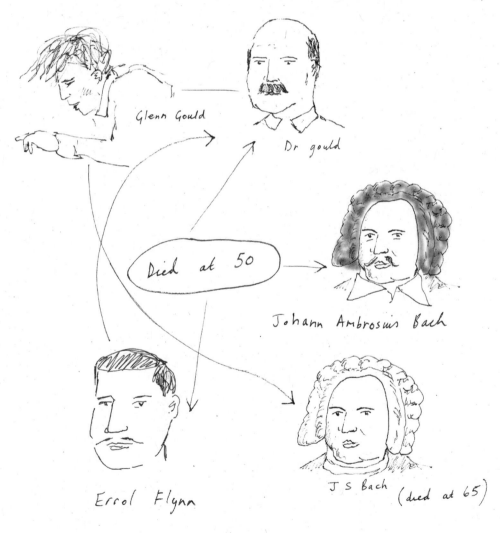

Glenn Gould

Dr gould

Died at 50

Johann Ambrosius Bach

Errol Flynn

J S Bach (died at 65)

J

Dear Old Father William,

I am noticing a certain morbidity creeping into your recent dispatches. Should I be concerned? Is it possible that you require more protein? I would be very happy to deliver something along the lines of poached chicken breast. Just say the word.

No word yet from my publisher friend. These things take a long time, or so I gather. In case you find yourself in the situation of giving interviews—as sometimes happens to authors!—here is an old and very dog-eared elocution manual. The pages have pretty much divorced the binding, but I think you might find something useful within.

There are a great many well-chewed mice in your garden, by the way. Your cats are enjoying the feline equivalent of salad days.

J. N.

Born on a Train

And now, repeat after Old Father William: *The trains in Spain are wracked with labour pains.*

•

Eleanora Duse, celebrated actress of the late nineteenth and early twentieth centuries and rival to Sarah Bernhardt, October 3, 1859, in a third-class carriage near Vigevano, Italy. She was born into her trade; her parents were itinerant players. She made the cover of *Time* magazine—the first woman ever so featured—on July 30, 1923, about nine months before her death (see *Died in a Hotel*).

•

Rod Carew, baseball player, October 1, 1945, in Panama. In those days of the colour bar, the train was segregated; because his mother was black, Carew was born in the less glamorous nether reaches of the conveyance. He was named for Dr. Rodney Cline, who happened to be on board and who supervised the delivery.

•

June Courington, professional bowler, 1921. Her father, Wiley Kelton, a ball player, was travelling by train through Georgia with his team at the time. Wives, evidently, were welcomed along, even those in advanced states of gravidity upon whom the rattle and roll might have a foreseeable effect. June bowled professionally during the 1950s, and in later years, according to her obituary in the *Chicago Sun-Times* (April 18, 2006), she built model ships out of bits of wood. She married Morris Courington, and is presumably the same Mrs. Morris (June) Courington quoted in *Time* (December 7, 1959), in an article describing the outrage in Deerfield, Illinois, about a developer's plan to sell one-fifth of the houses in a new subdivision to "Negroes." "It just can't happen in Deerfield," she said. "It just can't." (June is named as one of the concerned citizens who led a march to the high school gym, where she told the crowd of six hundred, "Some shyster came around and offered us about half what our house is worth. We called the real estate company and they wouldn't even accept our listing.")

•

Rudolf Nureyev, ballet superstar and international jet-setter, March 17, 1938, near Irkutsk, Siberia. Julie Kavanagh, in her 2007 biography, says that Nureyev's sister, Rosa, always called him, in a single breath, *Malchik kotoriy rodilsay v poezde:* the-boy-who-was-born-on-a-train. One of the many scholars Kavanagh quotes in her comprehensive book is Robert Conquest (see *Born in a Hotel*).

•

Tamara Toumanova, Russian prima ballerina and muse to George Balanchine and Leonide Massine, March 2, 1919, in a boxcar in Siberia. Her mother was a refugee from the revolution, fleeing to Shanghai to join her husband, an exiled czarist loyalist. Alongside Tania Riabouchinskaya and Irina Baranova, Toumanova was one of the three "Baby Ballerinas" who starred in Colonel W. de Basil's Ballet Russe de Monte Carlo round about 1932. She was known as "the Black Pearl of the Russian Ballet."

•

Maria von Trapp, January 26, 1905, in the train that was taking her mother to a clinic in Vienna. Praise the Lord for her safe delivery: who can imagine a world without *The Sound of Music?*

•

Movita Castaneda, actress, second wife of Marlon Brando, December 4, 1917, somewhere between Mexico and Arizona. She appeared in a 1935 version of *Mutiny on the Bounty;* Brando met his third wife while filming the 1962 *Bounty* remake. Irony makes the world go round.

{ **Rudolph Nureyev's sister always called him, in a single breath, "the-boy-who-was-born-on-a-train."** }

Alfredo Bevilacqua, Argentine composer, pianist, tango master, and charter member of the so-called Guardia Vieja, February 20, 1874, between Retiro and Olivos on the Ferro-Carril del Norte. He worked in Buenos Aires in the early days of the twentieth century, when the tango was still a demimonde phenomenon, an indulgence of stevedores, prostitutes, and gauchos taking a break from the pampas. His compositions include "Venus," "Minguito," and "Brisas del Sur."

Bisquick

+

Mickey Mouse

+

Maria Von Trapp

Born on a train

Lucie Eddie Campbell Williams, Baptist composer and educator, April 3, 1885, in a caboose, Duck Hills, Mississippi. Her father worked for the Mississippi Central Railroad and was killed in a train accident shortly after Lucie's birth. She was an early associate of Marian Anderson, and Mahalia Jackson and Ruth Davis were among the gospel singers who recorded her songs, which include "Footprints of Jesus," "My Lord and I," and "He'll Understand and Say Well Done."

Mickey Mouse, in 1928, somewhere between Kansas City and Los Angeles. Walt Disney wanted him christened "Mortimer"; his wife, Lillian, present for the birth, intervened and prevailed.

Catherine de Hueck Doherty, Catholic activist, naturalized Canadian, and candidate for canonization, August 15, 1896, in Nizhni Novgorod. She led a colourful, adventuresome life, eventually making her way to Toronto, where she founded a Catholic lay organization, Friendship House. She then set up a branch in New York, but scandalized her co-workers when she married Eddie Doherty, a well-known reporter and Academy Award–nominated screenwriter. They decamped for Canada, where nights are cold and celibacy is discouraged. In Combermere, Ontario, she founded the Madonna House Apostolate. Her case for canonization was opened shortly after her death in 1985.

•

Lorelei Lee, in 1923, one of the finest creations in all of American fiction. Anita Loos began writing about the blondes gentlemen prefer while travelling by rail from New York to Hollywood.

How to Elocute

The student should be careful to keep the body erect. A good voice depends upon it. An instrument, to produce a good tone, must be kept in tune. The practice of Position and Gesture will prove a valuable aid in physical culture, and in acquiring a graceful address. . . . Advance, retire, or change, with ease, except when the action demands energy, or marked decision. Adopt such positions only as consist of manly and simple grace, and change as the sentiment or subject changes, or as you direct attention to different parts of the audience. Avoid moving about, or "weaving," or moving the feet or hands while speaking.

TERROR   VENERATION—SUBMISSION   APPEAL TO HEAVEN   DEPRECATION

—A.A. Griffiths, *Lessons in Elocution* (1865)

Died on a Train

There is a balance to the universe, as Old Father William knows well, and just as life is now and then jounced into being on a train so, sometimes, does it gutter and fail.

•

Bess (Mrs. Harry) Houdini, February 11, 1943, on an eastbound train in the vicinity of Needles, California. For ten years after her husband's death, Mrs. Houdini held a séance on the roof of the Knickerbocker Hotel. Mr. Houdini never deigned to appear.

•

John Burroughs, conservation advocate, March 21, 1921, en route to California from the east. A Thoreau-like figure, he was an early disciple of Walt Whitman—indeed, he was a kind of Whitman look-alike, especially insofar as facial hair was concerned—and Whitman's first biographer. He evolved an important career as a writer, conservationist, and naturalist. Burroughs had an aphoristic gift, and was given to mining such nuggets as "I have discovered the secret of happiness—it is work, either with the hands or the head. The moment I have something to do, the draughts are open and my chimney draws, and I am happy"; and "Travel and society polish one, but a rolling stone gathers no moss, and a little moss is a good thing on a man."

•

Theodore Ritch, Russian tenor, 1943, in a transport train on the way to Auschwitz. Who could imagine a more shocking contrast to the event described in the *New York Times* on May 27, 1922? "His Majesty, the Shah of Persia, was the guest of honor at a dinner given this evening by Myron T. Herrick, American Ambassador to France. There was a special program of Russian music after the dinner. Special Russian numbers were sung by Mme. Spiridowitch, Prince Alexis Obolenski, Count Tolstoi and Theodore Ritch of the Chicago Opera Company."

•

Zerelda James Samuel, February 10, 1911, between Oklahoma City and San Francisco. The mother of Jesse and Frank James, she was said to be a woman of great verve and enterprise. After the deaths of her sons, she charged visitors a dollar a head for a tour of the family farm that included a viewing of the fireplace damaged when Pinkerton agents, seeking her outlaw sons, threw a bomb through the window. The bomb had killed her youngest son, Archie, and taken off Zerelda's arm. The capper of the tour was a visit to Jesse's grave in the front yard.

•

Edward McNamara, actor, November 10, 1944, while approaching Boston. He had a penchant for playing police officers in such films as *Arsenic and Old Lace, The Gay Sisters, The Palm Beach Story,* and *My Gal Sal.*

•

Jean Moulin, French resistance leader, July 8, 1943, apparently while being tortured by the Gestapo on a train somewhere between Paris and Berlin.

•

Harry Bateman, English-born mathematician, January 21, 1946. The long-time numbers avatar at the California Institute of Technology and author of *The Mathematical Analysis of Electrical and Optical Wave-motion,* and other such well-loved texts, was travelling from California to New York to receive an award from the Institute of Aeronautical Science.

•

Fats Waller, December 15, 1943, during a stop in Kansas City. While Tamara Toumanova was "the Black Pearl of the Russian Ballet," Waller was, according to Oscar Levant, "the Black Horowitz."

J

Dear Old Father William,

The Black Horowitz? Imagine. Fats Waller's
son, Maurice, who was very young when his
father died, wrote a biography of Fats—
I must see if I can find you a copy. He says
that, after the funeral, his ashes were scattered
over Harlem by a World War I pilot
known as the Black Ace: African American,
evidently. Though I have hunted high and
low for any reference to a pilot of that vintage,
race, and name, I can find nothing.
   I wonder if Waller might have meant
Eugene Bullard, a remarkable African
American man who lived much of his life in
France—a boxer and entertainer and, yes,
distinguished World War I pilot. He was
known as "the Black Swallow of Death."

I believe he ended his days as an elevator operator in the Rockefeller Center: a slower, gentler kind of aviation.

J.N.

P.S. The opera club meets next week; I'll make inquiries.

The Black List

The Black Horowitz. The Black Swallow of Death. Quite a number of African Americans of distinction were saddled with similar sobriquets, the obvious subtext being a kind of marvel at how such a manifestation of talent was possible in so unlikely a host: racism in the very diaphanous mask of benevolence.

Sissieretta Jones	The Black Adelina Patti
Granville Woods	The Black Thomas Edison
Nicky Barnes	The Black Godfather
Howard University	The Black Harvard
Spotswood Poles	The Black Ty Cobb
Buck Leonard	The Black Lou Gehrig
Josh Gibson	The Black Babe Ruth
Harriet Tubman	The Black Moses
Cooley High	The Black *American Graffiti*
Public Enemy	The Black Sex Pistols
Dr. José Jones	The Black Jacques Cousteau
Billy Dee Williams	The Black Clark Gable
Le Chevalier de Saint-George	The Black Mozart
August Wilson	The Black Shakespeare
C.L.R. James	The Black Plato
Shirley Verrett	La Negra Callas, to Italian opera lovers
Greenwood district of Tulsa, Oklahoma (also, the Jackson Ward district of Richmond, Virginia)	The Black Wall Street

Born in a Hotel

One of the few things in life over which we have no control is how and where our lives begin. Plainly, that reflects the situation of one's mother at the contractual moment, so to speak. Here is a list of some people who uttered their first cries in a hotel. Womb service, anyone?

•

Andre Gregory, actor, director, and subject of the film *My Dinner with Andre,* May 11, 1934, in a hotel in Paris.

•

Ludwig Bemelmans, author and illustrator of the *Madeline* books, among many others, April 27, 1898, in the hotel owned by his father.

•

James Hillman, Jungian therapist and author of several seminal new age texts, including *The Soul's Code,* 1926, in Atlantic City.

•

Robert Conquest, English historian and prominent author of books on Soviet history and politics, including *The Great Terror,* 1917, in a hotel in Malvern, to "a Virginian gentleman and a British mother" (*Guardian,* February 15, 2003).

•

Crown Prince Alexander of Yugoslavia, July 1945, in suite 212 of Claridge's Hotel. King Peter II had fled to London after being exiled from Yugoslavia in 1941. The suite was ceded to Yugoslavia for the occasion.

•

Austen Henry Layard, pioneering archaeologist and excavator of Nineveh and Nimrud, March 5, 1817, in a Left Bank hotel in Paris.

•

Barbara Cooney, Caldecott Medal–winning children's book illustrator, August 6, 1917, in room 1127 of the Hotel Bossert in Brooklyn, New York. When she received her first Caldecott in 1959, for *Chanticleer and the Fox,* she said, "I believe that children in this country need a more robust literary diet than they are getting... . It does not hurt them to read about good and evil, love and hate, life and death. Nor do I think they should read only about things that they understand. . . . A man's reach should exceed his grasp. So should a child's. For myself, I will never talk down to—or draw down to—children." Which remain words to live by.

Died in a Hotel

Just as there are those who check into this life in a hotel, there are those who check out. Nobel-winning playwright **Eugene O'Neill** deserves special mention as someone who did both. His last words are widely reported to have been "Born in a hotel room, and God dammit, died in one." He was born October 16, 1888, in a hotel on Broadway, and died November 27, 1953, in room 410 of the Shelton Hotel, Boston, now a dormitory of Boston University.

•

Eleanora Duse, actress, April 21, 1924, suite 524 of the Hotel Schenley, Pittsburgh. The hotel is now the William Pitt Union for the University of Pittsburgh (see also *Born on a Train*).

•

Anna Pavlova, ballerina, January 23, 1931, Hotel des Indes, the Hague. She became ill after her train was delayed by a rail accident and she spent an extended time in a cold carriage. Pneumonia settled in and she died three days later. Reporting her death, *Time* said, "On the third day she roused from a coma and spoke to Victor Dandré, her husband and accompanist. She thought she was herself again, high on her toes, poised for dancing. 'Play that last measure softly,' she said." Her ashes were on display in the Golders Green crematorium in London for seventy years, along with her ballet slippers. In 2001, after a long and unseemly tug-of-war, she was installed in the Novodevichy Cemetery in Moscow.

•

Max Baer, boxer, November 21, 1959, Roosevelt Hotel, Hollywood. (see also *Shaves Too Close for Comfort, Died at Fifty*).

•

John Philip Sousa, composer, novelist, bandmaster, and "March King," March 6, 1932, Abraham Lincoln Hotel, Reading, Pennsylvania.

•

Gram Parsons, musician, September 19, 1973, room 8 of the Joshua Tree Inn, Joshua Tree, California.

•

Oscar Wilde, November 30, 1900, room 16 of L'Hôtel, Paris. (see also *Other Awful Scandals Wrought by Artful Vandals*).

•

Janis Joplin, October 4, 1970, musician, room 105 of the Landmark Motor Hotel, Los Angeles (now the Highland Gardens Hotel).

•

Johnny Thunders, musician and New York Doll, April 23, 1991, room 37 of St. Peter House Hotel, New Orleans.

•

S.J. Perelman, humourist, October 17, 1979, room 1621 of the Gramercy Park Hotel, New York.

•

Warren G. Harding, sitting U.S. president, August 2, 1923, room 8064 of the Palace Hotel, San Francisco.

•

Anna Nicole Smith, courtesan, February 8, 2007, room 607 of the Seminole Hard Rock Hotel, Hollywood, Florida.

•

John Entwistle, musician June 27, 2002, room 658 of the Hard Rock Hotel, Las Vegas. Mr. Entwistle passed his last hours with a stripper named Alison Rowse. By way of cosmically balancing this tragic event, Britney Spears and Kevin Federline conceived their first child in this same hotel, room 248. Curiously, room 248 is also the meeting room of the Sperm Lab of Zhejiang University, in China.

•

D.W. Griffith, director, July 23, 1948, in the lobby of the Knickerbocker Hotel, Los Angeles.

•

William Frawley, actor, March 3, 1966, also in the lobby of the Knickerbocker Hotel. Mr. Frawley appeared as Fred Mertz on *I Love Lucy*, and opposite Fred MacMurray on *My Three Sons*.

•

Al Jolson, entertainer, October 23, 1950; cashed in his chips while playing cards in room 1221 of the St. Francis Hotel, San Francisco.

•

Delmore Schwartz, poet, July 11, 1966, in the lobby of the Times Square Hotel, New York.

•

Herbert Hoover, former U.S. president, October 20, 1964, suite 31A, Waldorf Towers, New York.

•

Nikola Tesla, scientist, January 7, 1943, room 3327 of the New Yorker Hotel, New York.

•

Pimp C, rapper, December 4, 2007, sixth floor of the Mondrian Hotel, Los Angeles.

•

Divine, actor, March 7, 1988, room 261 of the Regency Hotel, Los Angeles. According to the website "Find a death," Divine was last seen by his friends when, after dinner, he leaned over the balcony and sang "Arrivederci, Roma."

Divine Sings His Swan Song

•

Enrico Caruso, singer, August 2, 1921, Hotel Vesuvius, Naples. (see also *Sausages, Then and Now and Between Times, What a Grecian Earns Is Owed to a Nightingale, The Driving and the Driven*).

•

Camille Saint-Saëns, composer, December 16, 1921, Hotel Oasis, Algiers. A few minutes before his death, he had been singing arias by Verdi.

•

Giuseppe Verdi, composer, January 27, 1901, suite 105 of the Grand Hotel et de Milan.

•

Walter Benjamin, German literary critic and philosopher, September 27, 1940, in the Hotel Francia, Port Bou, on the Spanish/French border, perhaps a suicide and certainly while fleeing the Nazis. Benjamin's suitcase contained, it's said, a cherished literary work. The suitcase disappeared after his death: where it went and exactly what it contained remain tantalizing mysteries.

•

Gene Pitney, musician, April 5, 2007, seventh floor executive suite in the Hilton Hotel, Cardiff, Wales.

•

Coco Chanel, designer, January 10, 1971, in the suite where she had lived for more than thirty years, Ritz Hotel, Paris.

•

Pamela Churchill Harriman, diplomat, February 5, 1997, in the pool of the Ritz Hotel, Paris. Mrs. Harriman, who had a knack for marrying well, was known to her friends and admirers as the greatest courtesan of the twentieth century.

•

Caroline Blackwood, actress and writer, February 14, 1996, Mayfair Hotel, New York. Ms Blackwood was born into the Guinness family, and married the painter Lucien Freud, the pianist Israel Citkowitz, and the poet Robert Lowell (see *Last Drippings from the Sausage Pan*).

What Is It with Wrestlers?

Why should it be that so many buff and oiled warriors of the ring give up the ghost in a daily rental situation? It is disturbing and we do not want to be disturbed.

•

Eddie Guerrero died on November 13, 2005, at the Marriott City Centre Hotel in Minneapolis. His motto was, "I lie! I cheat! I steal!" His finishing move was the "Lasso from El Paso."

•

Rodney Anoa'i, also known as Yokozuna and Mr. Sumo, died October 23, 2000, in Liverpool, while a guest at the Moat House Hotel. Andy Russell, eulogizing Mr. Anoa'i in the English tabloid the *Sun,* speculated that the massive man's heart might have been pushed over the edge by a spider:

> Tour promoter Brian Dixon said the wrestler even had a clause about creepy-crawlies written into his contract. He added: "It stipulated that he had to have his dressing rooms and hotel rooms swept 30 minutes before he entered them to make sure there were no spiders. He was not frightened of anything he faced in the ring but I gather he had a lifelong phobia about spiders. It wasn't just big spiders like tarantulas—he was even scared of small money spiders."

His weight at death was 598 pounds. His finishing move was the "Banzai Drop."

•

Curt Hennig, a.k.a. Mr. Perfect, died on February 10, 2003, in the Homestead Suites, Brandon, Florida, a suburb of Tampa, apparently of a cocaine overdose. His finishing move was the "Perfect Plex."

Instructions for better living

How to Win at Wrestling

Do not let anything discourage you. Be GAME. Keep on trying. Until you are thrown both shoulders to the mat and the decision given against you, don't believe it possible for you to lose. If you get into a bad place use every strategy and effort to get away without too great an expense to strength and energy, yet at times it will require every ounce of muscle you possess, but DO NOT GIVE UP. BE GAME. BE GAME.

—*Farmer Burns School of Wrestling,*
Lessons in Wrestling and Physical Culture (1913)

•

André René Roussimoff, a.k.a. **André the Giant**, died January 27, 1993, in a hotel in Paris. He was in France attending his father's funeral. Samuel Beckett was reportedly a neighbour while André was growing up and would sometimes give him a ride to school. André's finishing move was the "Kneeling Belly to Belly Piledriver."

•

Here are some other finishing moves and the wrestlers who use or have used them:

Finishing Move	Wrestler
The Camel Clutch	Damien Demento
The Cobra Clutch	Barney Irwin, a.k.a. The Goon
Flying Forearm Smash	Nick "Big Bully" Busick
The Polish Hammer	John Rechner, a.k.a. Xanta Klaus
Running Shoulder Tackle	Peter Polaco, a.k.a. Aldo Montoya
The Stampede	Mike Hallick, a.k.a. Mantaur
Standing Knee Drop to the Head	Mike "Duke the Dumpster" Drose
The Stump Puller	Mike Shaw, a.k.a. Bastion Booger
Swinging DDT	Joe Scarpa, a.k.a. Chief Jay Strongbow
The Tomahawk Chop	Michael "Corporal" Kirchner
The Trash Compactor	Joseph Bednarski, a.k.a. Ivan Putski, a.k.a. Polish Power
A Trip to the Batcave	Merced Solis, a.k.a. Tito Santana

You CAN Take It with You

Before the sheen of positive thinking grows tarnished and dim, consider the following burials.

•

When **Dewaine Dutkowski** passed away, in Yellowknife, Northwest Territories, on June 12, 2007, his funeral arrangements were overseen by the workers and patrons of Harley's Hard Rock Saloon, where he had been a regular and earned for himself the affectionate nickname "Perv." He was a great favourite of the exotic dancers who performed there and, in his honour, the club's original brass pole was removed from the stage and broken into two parts. One half went into his coffin, and one half was used to decorate Mr. Dutkowski's headstone.

•

It's well known, and often reported, that Lauren Bacall placed into **Humphrey Bogart**'s urn a tiny gold whistle inscribed with a reference to the famous line from *To Have and Have Not:* "If you need anything, just whistle." Here are a few other examples of totems and charms that have accompanied the dead on their journeys, or at least as far down as six feet under.

Sofie Herzog's Bullet Necklace

- **Tiny Tim**, his ukulele.
- **Edith Piaf**, three stuffed animals: a rabbit, a squirrel and a lion.
- **Bob Marley**, a guitar, a soccer ball, a Bible, a ring that was a gift from Prince Asfa Wossen of Ethiopia, and a marijuana bud.
- **Wild Bill Hickok**, his rifle.
- **Arthur Prince**, a ventriloquist who died in 1948, was buried with his doll, Jim. "Arthur Prince & Jim" reads the gravestone.
- **Ernest Houston Johnson**. The first black student to attend Stanford University was buried with his Stanford diploma. He died in 1898 at the age of twenty-seven.
- **Sofie Dalia Herzog**. The first woman to serve as head surgeon for a major American railroad, she was buried with a necklace she had made from twenty-four bullets she'd extracted from the flesh of various patients over the years. She also had a notable collection of rattlesnake skins. She died in Houston on July 21, 1925.
- **Margaret Roper**, daughter of Sir Thomas More, had her father's severed head embalmed. (see also *A Highly Selective Survey of Pre-Decapitory Utterances*). It was buried with her nine years later, in 1544.
- **Anne Damer**, English sculptor (d. 1828), asked that she be buried with her apron and other tools of her trade, mallets and chisels and so on.
- **Queen Victoria**. Took remnants of Prince Albert and her Scottish retainer—some say husband— John Brown to earth with her: one of the former's robes, and a lock of the latter's hair.

•

Donahoe's Magazine, in 1886, carried a description of the "Order of the Buried Alive:"

> The Order of the Buried Alive in Rome, the Convent of the Sepolte Vivo, is a remnant of the Middle Ages in the life of to-day.... Communication with the convent is carried on through the "barrel," which fills an opening in the wall. Over the barrel is written: "Who will live contented within these walls, let her leave at the gate every earthly care." You knock at the barrel, which turns slowly around till it shows a section like that of an orange from which one of the quarters has been cut. You speak to the invisible sister, who asks your will; and she answers you in good Italian and cultivated intonation.... These nuns live on charity, keeping two Lents in the year— one from November to Christmas, the other the ordinary Lent of Catholic Christendom. Living, therefore, on charity, they may eat whatever is given to them, saving always "flesh meat" during the fasting time.... One of the pretty traditions of Rome is, that each sister has her day, when she throws a flower over the convent wall as a sign to her watching friends that she is still alive. When she has been gathered to the majority, the flower is not thrown, and the veil has fallen forever. They must be absolutely without food for twenty-four hours before they may ask help from the outside world; and when they have looked starvation in the face, then they may ring a bell, which means: "Help us! we are famishing!"

•

The Victorian novelist **Wilkie Collins** suffered from—or perhaps enjoyed— taphophobia, which is the fear of premature burial. So did **Hans Christian Andersen**. Collins carried a document asking for a second opinion in the case of his apparent death, and Andersen, when travelling, would leave a note by his bedside, advising anyone who found him that he was merely sleeping and wasn't to be mistaken for deceased. **Frédéric Chopin** was one of many who left instructions that his veins be opened at death so that there could be no chance of his waking up in the airless dark of a coffin.

This fear has not been diminished by modernity. On March 29, 2006, Martin Raymond, director of a trend-spotting think tank called the Future Laboratory, told the BBC that more and more people in South Africa, and elsewhere, were taking the "just in case" step of being buried with cell phones.

•

Courtesy of Jane Nurse, Old Father William is the happy keeper of a copy of *Black's Medical Dictionary,* the twenty-seventh edition, from 1967. The entry "Death, Signs of," includes these helpful suggestions for gauging the cessation of life:

> Most important for the immediate recognition of death are stoppage of the heart for five minutes, as listened for by placing the ear on the chest at the inner side of the left nipple, and cessation of breathing, as noted by observing that a mirror held before the mouth shows no haze, that a feather placed on the upper lip does not flutter, or that the reflection on the ceiling from a cup of water placed on the chest of a dead person shows no movement.

For some reason I find the business about the feather fluttering ever so slightly disturbing. Should I be wearing one on a delicate gold chain around my neck, come the day it's required for just this purpose?

J

Dear Old Father William,

Somewhere, somehow, I came upon a facsimile of Wilkie Collins's last will and testament, and was interested to note that he forbade the wearing of feathers to his funeral. Was that a usual stricture, or was it particular to him? Also, I wonder if you might want to add Anton Chekhov to your list of persons who died in hotels (July 15, 1904, Badenweiler, Germany).

I suggest this only because your editor might require a certain rigour and thoroughness. Have I mentioned yet that they're going to publish your book? I've always wondered what champagne looks like when decanted into a resealable bag. Now I know. Congratulations.

J.N.

Dear Jane Nurse,
I know this is meant to be good news,
so why do I feel a kind of dread? Did
you know that Chekhov's last words
were "It's a long time since I drank
champagne"?

O.F.W.

J

Dear Old Father William,

Do you want me to come in there
and slap you?

J.N.

Dear Jane Nurse,
And they shipped his body back to
Moscow in a refrigerated boxcar
marked "For Oysters Only."

O.F.W.

J

Dear Old Father William,

Feel free to let go of the morbidity
any old time now.

J.N.

Laid Low by a Bivalve

François Vatel, chef to Louis XIV and inventor of crème chantilly, ran himself through with a sword in 1671 rather than face the shame of a late-served meal when his order of oysters wasn't delivered.

•

Edward Wertheimer, of the well-to-do London family whose portraits were painted by John Singer Sargent, died on his honeymoon, in Paris, after eating a bad oyster.

•

Bernd Rosemeyer, German racing car driver, was hospitalized for six weeks in 1935, after eating a bad oyster.

•

Michael Winner, English director (*Death Wish 2* and *Death Wish 3*) and food critic for the *Sunday Times,* very nearly died after eating a bad oyster in Barbados, January 2007.

•

Mariah Carey had to reschedule the Boston leg of her 2000 "Rainbow" tour, as well as her Toronto concert, when she ate a bad oyster in Atlanta. (Like many other bad things that went down in Atlanta, it was presumably, after a time, gone with the wind.)

•

Wilbur Wright, of the flying Wright brothers, contracted typhus and died after eating a bad oyster in Boston in 1912.

•

And this tale of fowl play, from the *Corpus Christi Caller* (November 23, 1884), suggests that not only humans are susceptible to harm from oysters; nor is ingestion the only cause of danger:

The curiosity of the season was exhibited at the Caller office last week by Mr. W.S. Halsey. It was a wild duck caught and killed by an oyster. It is the first time we have ever seen or heard of an oyster successfully bagging game, but the evidence of this incident was too strong to be doubted. The duck was a large and full grown one that had recently come from the north to enjoy our winter climate. It was of the diving species, which inhabit the bays till the spring, when they return north. The duck had evidently seen a large fat oyster enjoying a drink of fresh water in its freedom on the bottom of the bay. When the oyster feeds it opens its shell wide till the full oyster is plainly visible. A sight of such a morsel was too much for the duck. He made a headlong plunge, inserting his bill between the oyster's open shells. Like a flash and with the power of a vise the shells closed on the duck's beak. Then came the struggle for life. The oyster, which was quite a large one, was dragged from its bed with three smaller ones clinging to it—the cluster being heavy enough to keep the duck's head under water. In this way the duck drowned. Its buoyancy was sufficient to float with the oysters, and thus drifted near the dock where it was captured by Mr. Halsey. When taken out of the water the animal heat had not left the duck. The oyster still clung to the duck's beak and with such force as to mash it considerably. This species of duck is fond of oysters and mussels and no doubt many are thus caught and anchored to the bottom of the bay in their eagerness to capture fat oysters.

How to Chase a Wild Goose

When preparing to chase the wild goose, avoid any clothing that is light or dark as you would a pestilence; there is only one thing worse than something black about your person, and that is something white. Many a good grey goose has had his life saved because his chaser wore a linen collar. If you see geese coming towards you and there is no cover at hand, throw yourself flat on your back, pull your cap well over your forehead, clutch a handful of grass or anything else available and put it over the lower part of your face, hide your hands—and then lie motionless as a log. Finally, when stalking grey geese you will always find one bird, a gander, acting as sentry, his head up, his neck as straight as a poker. Make him the special object of your stalk. Do not stir a muscle while an eye of his is turned towards you. Should he detect the slightest movement, a movement which the feeding and resting birds would not notice, you are done for.

—L.H. De Visme Shaw, "The Wild Goose and Its Chase,"
Badminton Magazine (1900)

Dear Jane Nurse,
Because really, it is just a
wild goose chase, isn't it?
O.F.W.

J

Dear Old Father William,

A chase after what?

J.N.

Dear Jane Nurse,
Glory. Wealth. Celebrity. Everything
that's egregious. Everything I dodge.
                              O.F.W.

J

Dear Old Father William,

It's a book, not a porn site. There's
very little chance that anyone will
ever see it.

J.N.

Dear Jane Nurse,
Ah. How do I end it?
O.F.W.

Dear Old Father William,

Just stop chasing the goose.

J.N.

All His Geese Were Swans,
Except When His Swans Were Geese

On April 21, 1915, the Finnish composer Jean Sibelius, a troubled, restless soul who wrestled with many demons, went out to commune with nature. He heard a clamour in the sky above him. He looked up and saw a flight of sixteen swans. The pattern they made as they reticulated the refulgent blue, and their raucous trumpeting, inspired the theme that became the finale of his Fifth Symphony.

On April 22, 1932, a flock of fifty-two wild geese was struck by lightning while flying over Elgin, Manitoba. Any who looked up at that moment, who happened to see the flash and hear the crack that followed, and who then had to dodge the pelting birds, would surely have seen something to rank among the most remarkable sights of his or her life. But most of the citizens of that tiny town would have had their heads down, as mostly we do. It's a defensive posture. Things happen all the time, every second of our lives, that could dazzle the daylights out of us. We could never accommodate it all. We'd fry up, out of sheer delight. The geese were gathered—not precooked, as one might suppose—and distributed to everyone in town: Manitoba manna, direct from Heaven.

Swans flew over Sibelius, and Sibelius made music. Geese flew over Elgin, and the Elginites made dinner. There's room for both in this life. One must have art and one must have nosh. The mind needs a place to live, and the body is its only real choice.

On March 8, 1941, shortly before she filled her pockets with stones and walked into the Ouse, Virginia Woolf wrote in her diary, "And now with some pleasure, I find that it is seven; and must cook dinner. Haddock and sausage meat. I think it's true one gains a certain hold on haddock and sausage by writing them down."

It was with sausage that we began, was it not, Jane Nurse? In which case, for now, I think we're done. At the risk of mixing meat-aphors, let's say this goose is caught. Now, for the cooking.

Go, little book.

Acknowledgements

Thanks to Sharon Kish, Brad Wilson, Noelle Zitzer, and everyone at HarperCollins, to Meg Masters and Sarah Wight, to Charles Checketts, to Dean Cooke, and most particularly to Henry Welby, the Hermit of Grub Street, and to Jane Nurse.